Top Level
Cookery for Two

The author grew up in Welwyn in Hertfordshire, and spent most of her holidays working in small family-run hotels in France. She acquired an interest in cookery, and gained much useful cooking experience. After university she spent two years in Spain and it was there that the idea for this cookery book came about.

The author recently qualified as a solicitor, and now lives in London.

Lynda Goetz

Top Level Cookery for Two

NEW ENGLISH LIBRARY

Acknowledgements

My special thanks to my friend Barbara Addison for her help with the typing. Thanks also to AMC for the loan of the electric typewriter.

A New English Library Original Publication, 1981

First NEL Paperback Edition July 1981

NEL Books are published by
New English Library Limited,
Barnard's Inn, Holborn,
London EC1N 2JR.

Printed in Great Britain by
Cox & Wyman, Reading, Berks

0 450 05200 1

Contents

For my parents
even though my father is not all that fond of garlic!

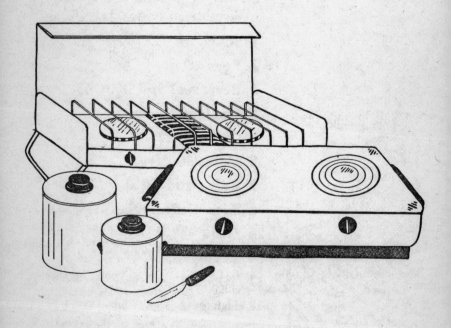

Foreword

What on earth should we call it? 'All on Top'? 'Simple Extravaganza for Two'? 'Look! No Oven'? We racked our brains for ages and I'm still not sure that the one we finally chose conveys all I would have liked to convey in the title, but since you've got as far as reading this, I suppose it can't be too bad!

When we first arrived in Spain, where we lived for two years, I was surprised when involved in the business of flat hunting, to find that every time I went to look at a cooker and opened what I thought was the oven door, that I was staring at an enormous orange butane gas container! Not a single one of the flats we saw had an oven and the one we ended up with was no exception. We were therefore forced to rethink much of our cooking, which led me in the end to produce this book, in the hopes of inspiring others who think that it is not easy to cook interesting dishes on the top of the cooker. We discovered fairly rapidly that the Spaniards rarely use an oven — which explains why they didn't see the necessity for them in flats they were letting.

The recipes are, however, by no means all Spanish; many are based on French cookery. I won't go as far as to say that France is where I acquired an interest in cookery, because that was acquired before, but I did learn a good deal during my various working holidays there. Two places in particular spring to mind — a small hotel in a village near Grasse and a family's country house in another small village near Nice. In the former, I particularly remember learning how to cook good *pommes frites* and how to make the radishes look attractive for the *salade niçoise;* in the latter I have memories of peeling vast quantities of pears for stewing and of excellent *ratatouille* (which also involved me in a lot of peeling and chopping). I suppose I should also mention a grape-picking holiday in the St Emilion district; but then with all the will in the world, one can't produce the flavour of steaks cooked over a charcoal fire by using a frying pan on a gas ring!

The basic ideas behind this little cookery book are fun and imagination. I hope it will appeal to many people, but particularly to those who are prepared to experiment and would like a few ideas to help them on their way. As none of the recipes need an oven it should be especially useful to those who are limited to one or two gas rings, in a bed-sit, caravan or boat for example. You'll be amazed at the number of interesting and varied recipes there are. It should also prove a good companion to those who are catering for themselves on the Continent, since many of the ingredients are cheaply and readily available in France, Spain and most Mediterranean countries. Explore the local markets!

For this reason, many of the recipes are not cheap. Many include wine and some vegetables such as aubergines and artichokes which are quite expensive here. However, they can be obtained, by those who wish to try and many, such as courgettes, are becoming commoner and much cheaper as they are increasingly grown in this country. In any case it is still an awful lot cheaper than going out to dinner! Thinking along these lines it is also worth noting that a number of these dishes are composite and are therefore at least economical on the washing up and fuel!

There are, in fact, also a number of nourishing and economical recipes, using rice and pasta and dried vegetables such as lentils and haricot beans which have long been neglected in the English cookery repertoire. As many of these dishes come in the one-pot category they need only one ring. However, if you are really managing on only one ring it is possible with good organisation to cook two dishes and serve both hot, as long as you work out which of the two is most easily reheated and I discuss this in the notes on page 10.

As far as the wine goes, I suggest that you keep any remainders you have in a bottle in the kitchen so that whenever a recipe calls for wine it does not necessarily entail opening a new bottle.

As I said earlier, one of the basic ideas of this book is imagination and for this reason I wouldn't like to think that those of you using these recipes were sticking rigidly to what I suggest. There is no baking, which is the one branch of cookery where quantities are vital, so omit what you don't like; add what you do like. It's all part of the fun of cooking! I hope that once the basics are mastered you'll feel free to adapt the recipes as you wish. As the title indicates most of the recipes are for two people, except where there is information to the contrary, but the portions are fairly generous. If you are using any of the recipes for a dinner party they can simply be adapted accordingly.

The quantities are given first in metric weights and then with the rough equivalent in Imperial. The approximate conversions in the recipes are quite adequate for this type of cookery. A conversion table is given on page 16.

As an indication of how long it is going to take you to cook and prepare these dishes I have noted at the top of each recipe approximate cooking and working times. Working time is *not* simply preparation time, which I feel is often misleading, but the time the cook needs to actually spend in the kitchen both in preparing the food for cooking and in overseeing operations like sautéing, making a roux, warming milk etc. I hope this will be considered a helpful inclusion.

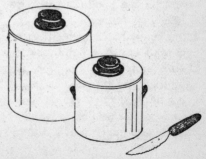

Some notes on cooking on one or two rings

So as not to repeat myself throughout the book, I am giving at the outset some hints on how to organise your cooking if you are limited to only one or two rings.

Obviously, the composite dishes, such as the several rice dishes given, pose no problems and are ideal for such a situation. What, however, if you want to cook, for example, a main meat dish, such as pork chops, plus chips and vegetables? In such a case, the best thing to do is first to fry the chips (see page 00) in very hot deep fat until they are a pale golden colour. At this point they should be removed from the fat, put aside and salted. Meanwhile, if you have two rings the meat and the vegetables can be cooked. If you are managing on only one, then the vegetables should be cooked, drained and a knob of butter added. When the meat is ready, the oil for deep-frying, which will still be warm, is reheated and the chips put back. Within a minute (as long as the fat is really hot) they will be a beautiful golden brown and nicely crisp on the outside. Whilst serving these out, the vegetables with their coating of butter may be reheated and the whole meal served hot. If the meat has perhaps cooled slightly it too can be briefly re-warmed.

The order in which these arrangements are made will depend largely on the dish that is being cooked. A casserole, for example, can easily be reheated, but a piece of steak must be fried just before it is served. When dealing with pasta it is usually best to reheat the sauce, although in the case of a dish such as Carmela's Macaroni (see page 120) the pasta and the sauce may be reheated together.

Certain things such as rice can, of course, be kept warm or be reheated in a pan or colander balanced on top of another pan in which something is being cooked. This will depend on the pans in use. The steam from vegetables being boiled can also be used to actually cook another dish, such as the fish on page 90.

In the summer, salads provide an excellent side dish which doesn't require any cooking and which form a good accompaniment to the main course. I include several variations on the salad theme – salads need not be just boring bits of limp lettuce with a piece of tomato stuck on top!

You still think you'd rather have potatoes with your meals but are not too sure you fancy the juggling and balancing acts which appear to be involved? Try putting the potatoes and other vegetables in the casserole and cooking them all together as in the Super Stew (see page 46) or the Castilian Lamb dish (see page 59). Alternatively, if you feel you need some carbohydrate to fill you up, why not try the continental habit of eating bread with a meal? Choose crispy rolls – slices of pre-packaged bread are not exactly the same thing!

Many of the dishes given here are interesting and different enough for dinner parties – which, believe it or not you can do even with only one ring if you are well organised. I give at the back some suggested menus. The few desserts I have included are simple and require little or no cooking. They are all ideal for occasions when you are entertaining in that they can be prepared in advance. In fact, they are not on the whole things you would do every day. I tend myself to use fresh fruit as a dessert on normal occasions. The starters I have included come into the same category as the desserts.

A list of spices and herbs

Spices

Cardamom The seed capsules of Indian plants washed and dried in the sun. The black seeds inside have a sharp lemony flavour. Use seeds whole for curries, finely ground in pastries, sweet sauces and cakes. Believed by the Arabs to be an aphrodisiac!

Caraway Used in bread and cakes as well as savoury dishes such as goulash. Caraway seeds are the dried fruits of an umbelliferous plant.

Chilli powder Like curry powder a mixture of ingredients. It is usually made up of different kinds of hot peppers (capsicums), cumin seeds, dried garlic and oregano; all finely ground. Much used in Mexican cookery.

Chilli The dried pod of a Mexican type of hot capsicum.

Cinnamon This spice is made from the dried inner bark of a tree that grows in Ceylon. Very good in cakes, biscuits and apple dishes. Excellent in mulled wine, and its sweet fragrant flavour is also an interesting addition to fresh fruit salad and to some savoury dishes.

Clove Dried flower buds from the East Indian tree Eugenia Aromatica. It has a highly aromatic scent and should be used sparingly. Can also be obtained ground. Whole cloves can be used for pickling, sticking in hams and in mulled wine, whilst ground cloves can be used in cakes and also in some meat dishes.

Coriander The seed of a parsley plant which grows in Southern Europe and Asia Minor with a sweet yet tart flavour. Used in curries and also in Moroccan dishes. The plant itself can also be used.

Cumin seed Another important curry spice. A warm pungent spice used extensively in Oriental and Mexican foods. Very good in dried bean dishes. Can also be added to rice whilst it is cooking to give a subtle flavour.

Curry powder A blend of herbs and spices. Commercial varieties vary in content and quality. True connoisseurs have special formulae for different dishes. As a compromise the commercial curry powders can be supplemented.

Ginger The rhizome of a Far Eastern plant which must be cleaned, scraped and boiled before it is dried to give us the buff-coloured root ginger. Ground ginger is creamy white. Very pungent but useful in both sweet and savoury dishes.

Mustard Imported by the Romans into Gaul where it quickly found favour, it now grows well throughout Europe. English mustard is a mixture of powdered black and white mustards with a little turmeric to give colour. Can be used by itself but is also good to flavour sauces and salad dressing.

Nutmeg Another East Indian spice. It is the dried fruit kernel of the tree, from which *mace* is also obtained. Both have a similar delicate aromatic flavour. Good in sweet dishes, such as egg custard but also useful with fish and vegetables in a cream sauce. Used quite frequently in Italian savoury dishes.

Paprika or **red pepper** Paprika features a great deal in Spanish, French, Hungarian and Moroccan cookery. Note when buying it that there are various kinds and that it does make a difference to the finished dish. It is no good therefore making Hungarian goulash with Spanish paprika, or Spanish Cocido with Hungarian paprika. Also note that there is mild or sweet red pepper and hot red pepper – which can be very hot!

Pepper This is the most widely used spice, particularly in England. Both black and white pepper are obtained from the fruit of a jungle vine now grown all over the tropical Far East. For black pepper the berries are picked when unripe and dried. For white they are picked when about to turn from green to red. The black is more aromatic and should, if possible, always be freshly ground.

Saffron The most expensive of all spices. It is made from the stigma of a small crocus. The best is grown in Spain. Adds a very distinctive but delicate flavour to rice and fish and also meat dishes.

Turmeric Made from the dried and ground root of an East Indian plant. Gives a rich orangey-yellow tinge to food. Used in curries and pickle.

Herbs

Basil An aromatic herb used in European cooking, particularly in tomato dishes. Fresh basil is especially good with a tomato salad. It requires quite a lot of sun to grow well.

Bayleaf The true laurel with which the ancients crowned their heroes. Bayleaf is very good for seasoning soups, stews and fish and is one of the three herbs which go to make up bouquet garni.

Bouquet garni Used a great deal in French cookery. In English it was known as a 'faggot of herbs'. It consists of bayleaf, a sprig of thyme and a small spray of parsley or several parsley stalks, which have more flavour and also the advantage of not disintegrating with long, slow cooking.

Fennel A herb native to Britain. It is particularly used in fish cookery.

Garlic In ancient Greece one was denied access to the temple after eating garlic! Nowadays no such sanctions exist, but do be careful if your best friends don't eat it. It is a bulb divided up into what are known as cloves. A clove is not, as I once overheard a shop assistant informing a poor unsuspecting customer, the whole bulb! An extremely useful herb in many savoury dishes.

Mint This is really a generic name, designating a group of perennial labiate herbs including basil and rosemary, but also more particularly the spearmint used for culinary purposes. Frequently added to boiled peas and potatoes but can also add an interesting flavour to salads, stews and punches.

Marjoram A herb used in stews and with poultry. This is the generic name and there are various kinds.

Oregano A type of wild marjoram much used in Continental cookery and which gives the distinctive flavour to such things as Italian pizzas.

Parsley There are several different types of parsley although the one most commonly seen in this country is the Italian or curly-leaved parsley. The origins of parsley are not really known, but it was introduced into this country in Tudor times. It is one of the ingredients in bouquet garni and also an extremely useful garnish. Its flavour and colour add a finishing touch to many dishes.

Rosemary A very fragrant herb, so be careful not to overdo it. It should be used sparingly. If at all possible it should be removed before serving the dish, as the spiky little leaves can be unpleasant if eaten. Good with lamb.

Tarragon Native to most Mediterranean countries. It is used to flavour vinegar and pickles, but can also be used in meat dishes and especially chicken.

Thyme An old favourite of the English herb garden. It is a very useful herb with a distinctive flavour. It is the third herb which makes up a bouquet garni.

Weights and measures

In the recipes I have given the quantities in metric measurements first, and then followed these by an approximate Imperial equivalent. Exact conversions between these two systems of measuring do not give convenient working amounts as 1 oz is actually 28.35 g, and 1 fl oz equals 35.5 ml. For ease I have taken 1 oz to equal 25 g, and 1 fl oz to equal 25 ml, making adjustments to keep as near the equivalent as possible. See the tables below.

Solids

Imperial (Ounces)	Metric (Recommended equivalent in grams)
1	25
2	50
3	75
4 ($\frac{1}{4}$ lb)	100
5	150
6	175
7	200
8 ($\frac{1}{2}$ lb)	225
9	250 ($\frac{1}{4}$ kg)
10	275
11	300
12 ($\frac{3}{4}$ lb)	350
13	375
14	400
15	425
16 (1 lb)	450

Liquids

Imperial (Fluid ounces)	Metric (Recommended equivalent in millilitres)
1	25
5 ($\frac{1}{4}$ pint)	125
10 ($\frac{1}{2}$ pint)	250
15 ($\frac{3}{4}$ pint)	350
20 (1 pint)	500 ($\frac{1}{2}$ litre)
40 (2 pints)	1000 (1 litre)

Spoons (Level)

$\frac{1}{2}$ teaspoon 2.5 ml	1 tablespoon 15 ml
1 teaspoon 5 ml	(Australian tablespoon: 20 ml)

An Australian cup holds 250 ml which for convenience in this book equals $\frac{1}{2}$ pint.

Note: When cooking follow one set of measurements only; do not mix them.

1 Soups

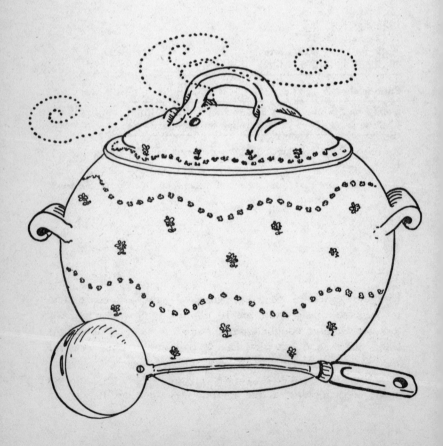

Soups are on the whole extremely simple to make and yet give such rewarding results. The selection here includes a couple which are or can be served cold, some main course soups and an interesting Greek soup which has a similar base to that used in the sauce for the Stuffed Cabbage Leaves on page 143. The quantities I have given in several cases are sufficient for four as a starter. There are two reasons for this: firstly, all these soups can be kept in a sealed container in the fridge for several days, and secondly, a good bowl of soup with some bread and cheese makes a very acceptable meal, but generally in such a case where there is no main course, the extra soup goes down very well!

Cream of vegetable soup

This soup can basically be made of any vegetables you have around and will come out with a slightly different flavour every time. Any leftover cooked vegetables can also be added just before you purée the soup.

Serves 4 Cooking time 1 hour Working time 20 minutes

½ kg (1 lb) vegetables (e.g.
 carrots, potatoes, onions, celery,
 cabbage, Brussels sprouts,
 turnips, leeks etc.)
30 g (good oz) butter

½ litre (1 pint) chicken stock
salt and pepper
bouquet garni
milk
1 tablespoon flour or cornflour
 (optional)
2 tablespoons cream (optional)

Dice the vegetables. Melt the butter in a large saucepan, add the vegetables and sauté for 10 minutes. Add the stock, salt and pepper and bouquet garni. Bring to the boil, lower the heat, cover and simmer for 45 minutes. When all the vegetables are tender, either put the soup through a sieve or vegetable mill or into an electric blender to obtain a smooth purée. The thickness of the soup at this stage will depend on the proportion of root vegetables such as potatoes, carrots and turnips. It may be thinned down by the addition of some milk to achieve the desired consistency, or the soup can be 'stretched' in any case by thickening with cornflour and then adding extra liquid. If thickening, don't forget to blend the flour or cornflour with a little cold liquid before adding it to the soup. Cook gently for a further 5-10 minutes. The milk will already have given the soup a creamy flavour, but a little extra butter may be added at this stage and the cream stirred in just before serving.

Note: If you prefer, the soup can be left as it is without making a purée, in which case the milk should be omitted and a little extra stock may be required.

Carrot soup

Cooking time 45 minutes Working time 15 minutes

½ kg (1 lb carrots)	½ litre (1 pint) chicken stock
1 onion	1 teaspoon sugar
1 medium potato	salt and pepper
50 g (2 oz) butter	chopped parsley

Dice the carrots, onion and potato. Melt half the butter in a pan until foaming, add the vegetables and fry gently for 5 minutes. Put in the stock and sugar and season with salt and pepper. Bring to the boil, lower the heat, cover and simmer for 30-40 minutes or until the carrots and potato are soft. Either sieve or put into a blender to make a purée. Mix in the remaining butter and serve sprinkled with a little chopped parsley.

Note: If the soup is too thick, extra water or stock may be added. The thickness of these type of soups depends a great deal on the quality and quantity of potatoes, so it is difficult to be exact about the stock.

Tomato soup

This is a very simple soup to make and has a very refreshing flavour.

Cooking time 30 minutes Working time 15 minutes

1 kg (2 lb) tomatoes
½ onion
25 g (1 oz) butter or 1 tablespoon olive oil
1-2 teaspoons sugar

salt
freshly milled pepper
milk or water
chopped parsley or mint

First skin the tomatoes by pouring boiling water over them and leaving them for a minute. This makes the skins easy to remove. Chop the tomatoes and the onion. Heat the butter or oil in a pan and fry the onion until softened. Add the tomatoes, sugar, salt and freshly milled pepper. Cover and cook gently for 20-25 minutes, then pass through a sieve or an electric blender. Thin out to the required consistency with milk or water and return to the pan to reheat before serving, sprinkled with chopped parsley or mint.

Note: A little cream turns this soup into a real luxury!

Potage bonne femme

Serves 4 Cooking time 45 minutes Working time 20 minutes

2 large leeks
1 carrot
2 large potatoes
25 g (1 oz) butter
1 litre (2 pints) water

1 teaspoon sugar
salt
freshly milled pepper
chopped chives, chervil or parsley

Clean the leeks by cutting off the root part and the very top leaves. Now cut the top part two ways in order to be able to clean it thoroughly and get rid of any mud that remains. Clean under running water. Slice finely. Clean and dice the carrots.

Peel and dice the potatoes. Melt the butter in a pan and sauté the leeks and carrots. Add the potatoes, the water, sugar, salt and freshly milled pepper. Bring to the boil, lower the heat, cover and simmer for 30-35 minutes or until the vegetables are all tender. Sieve or put into a blender. If the soup is too thick at this stage add a little milk until it reaches the desired consistency. Adjust the seasoning. Serve sprinkled with chopped chives, chervil or parsley.

Note: This soup is also excellent served cold. The carrot is usually omitted and some heavy cream added while the soup is being chilled. Served like this it is known as Vichyssoise.

Mushroom soup

Cooking time 20 minutes Working time 20 minutes

200 g (8 oz) mushrooms	½ litre (1 pint) milk
½ small onion	a few tablespoons chicken stock
30 g (good oz) butter	salt and pepper
1 dessertspoon flour	

Chop the mushrooms and the onion finely and sauté very gently in the butter for 5-10 minutes. Blend in the flour and add the milk and the chicken stock, stirring constantly with a wooden spoon. Season with salt and pepper. Cook until it has thickened.

Tomato and celery soup

This is really a 'cheats' recipe, but is very useful as a way of making a rather uninspiring can of soup into something more interesting.

Cooking time 15-20 minutes Working time 15 minutes

1 small onion
1-2 sticks celery
25 g (1 oz) butter
1 can tomato soup
1 dessertspoon lemon juice

½ teaspoon sugar
1 dessertspoon chopped parsley
pinch basil (optional)
salt and pepper

Chop the onion and celery very finely and sauté in the butter until soft and just turning golden. Add the remaining ingredients, bring to simmering point and simmer for 5 minutes. Season with salt and pepper to taste.

Cream of lettuce soup

This is a delicious soup with a delicate flavour. It will probably have your friends guessing if served at a dinner party! I must confess that I had never even considered making lettuce soup until one summer I was left by myself to look after my parents' home for three weeks. After a week, during which I had salad every day, I was desperately wondering what else I could possibly do with the surfeit of lettuces on my hands. It was pretty obvious that even if I ate nothing but salad, served lettuce as a side salad at all my dinner parties and even served cooked lettuce as a vegetable (delicious, incidentally; see page 148) I was still not going to be able to use up sufficient to stop half of them going to seed. This soup proved the ideal answer and could be stored in the freezer for the family's return. Assuming you are not faced with such problems this is nevertheless a soup worth making.

Serves 4 Cooking time 35-40 minutes Working time 20 minutes

1 medium onion
2 large heads lettuce
25 g (1 oz) butter
1 rounded dessertspoon flour
½ litre (1 pint) milk

½ litre (1 pint) chicken stock (or made up chicken noodle soup)
salt and pepper
fresh chopped mint

Finely chop the onion. Wash and drain the lettuce and with a sharp knife shred the lettuce finely. Melt the butter in a saucepan, add the onion and cook gently for 2-3 minutes. Add the lettuce and fry a further few minutes, then cover the pan and sweat the vegetables in the butter. After 5 minutes draw the pan off the heat, sprinkle on the flour and mix well. Heat the milk and pour over the vegetables. Add the stock and season with salt and pepper. Bring to the boil, lower the heat, cover and simmer for 20-25 minutes, then blend in a blender. If you do not possess such a thing you'll have to do it the hard way and put it through a fine sieve! This can be made slightly easier if you put it through a vegetable mill first. Adjust the seasoning and serve with chopped mint.

Note: For something slightly different try serving this soup chilled.

Onion soup

Cooking time 35 minutes Working time 25 minutes

½ kg (1 lb) onions	salt and pepper
75 g (3 oz) butter	toasted rounds bread
1 tablespoon flour	grated Gruyère cheese
1 litre (2 pints) chicken stock	

Peel and slice the onions thinly. Melt the butter in a large pan, add the onions and fry gently until they are golden. Blend in the flour, then stir in the stock. Season with salt and pepper. Bring to the boil, lower the heat, cover and simmer for 20 minutes. Adjust the seasoning. Place the toasted rounds of bread in soup bowls, pour in the soup and sprinkle the grated cheese on top.

Note: If you have not got access to a toaster, bread can always be toasted on the top if you have the patience to hold it on a fork over the heat.

Sweet corn chowder

Serves 4 Cooking time 40 minutes Working time 30 minutes

2-4 rashers streaky bacon	½ litre (1 pint) water
2 potatoes	salt and pepper
1 large onion	½ litre (1 pint) milk
1 stick celery	1 tablespoon flour
1 green pepper	1 small tin sweetcorn, drained
1 bayleaf	chopped parsley

Remove the rind from the bacon and dice. Peel and dice the potatoes and the onion. Chop the celery and the green pepper. Fry the bacon gently using a little oil or butter if its own fat is insufficient. Add the onion and celery and fry until a golden brown, then add the green pepper, potatoes, the bayleaf and the water. Season with salt and pepper to taste. Bring to the boil, lower the heat, cover and simmer until the potato is tender. Use a little of the milk to blend with the flour and add this to the chowder whilst heating the rest of the milk. Add the heated milk and the drained sweetcorn to the chowder. Simmer long enough to heat the sweetcorn, then serve scattered with chopped parsley.

Serving suggestion: Serve with fresh brown or French bread. This soup is substantial and makes a good main course soup.

Consommé al Jerez

Jerez, as most people know is where the sherry comes from and is the word which was corrupted into our English word 'sherry'. This soup is a very common starter in Spain, especially in Andalucia, the region in which Jerez is situated.

The recipe can be made in two ways. There is the old-fashioned way which consists in boiling up the bones of a chicken or other meat with water, an onion, a carrot and seasoning and then straining it to get the consommé.

Alternatively, there is the instant modern method, which consists simply in using a couple of stock cubes to make the consommé. The former is useful if you do happen to have bones left over and the other very convenient if you are short of time and/or money. It is also a good meal for slimmers. If using stock cubes it helps pep up the flavour if a few herbs are sprinkled in whilst cooking. If possible the consommé should be served with a small sprig of fresh mint in each bowl. On the table have a bottle of very pale dry sherry, 'fino'. Each person adds a spoonful to their soup. This addition really transforms a very ordinary soup into something special.

Consommé al Jerez is a favourite during the Feria in Sevilla. It is very warming in the early hours of the morning when you have been on the go all night!

For the purists who wish to use proper stock I give a recipe below. For two people it is often not practical to prepare stock so the quantity I give makes a larger amount for any special occasions.

Stock for consommé

Cooking time 2-3 hours Working time 10-15 minutes

¼ kg (½ lb) shin of beef or chicken carcass
1 large onion
1-2 carrots
1 stick celery
¼ kg (½ lb) each veal and beef bones

cold water (1½-2 litres, 3-4 pints) to cover
bouquet garni
salt
a few peppercorns

If making beef stock, brown the beef in a small quantity of fat. Chop the onion, carrots and celery, then add the vegetables to the beef and brown. Add the bones, water, bouquet garni, salt and peppercorns. Bring to the boil, lower the heat, cover and simmer for 2-3 hours. Strain, and when completely cold, skim off the fat.

If making chicken stock, brown the vegetables and add the chicken carcass with the water together with the remaining ingredients. Proceed as with the beef stock.

Reheat and adjust the seasoning.

Corn curry soup

This soup is unbelievably simple to make and yet is as nourishing and as interesting as soups that take a great deal more time and effort.

Cooking time 10 minutes Working time 2 minutes

1 tin creamed sweetcorn
¼ litre (½ pint) milk
¼ litre (½ pint) stock (1 stock cube and water)

salt and pepper
1 level teaspoon curry powder

Pour the creamed sweetcorn into a saucepan. Add the milk and stock and stir well. Season with salt, pepper and curry powder and heat slowly just before serving. Once it has reached boiling point it is ready to serve.

Greek egg and lemon soup

Cooking time 20 minutes Working time 5 minutes

½ litre (1 pint) stock
salt
25 g (1 oz) long-grain rice

1 egg
juice of ½ lemon
salt and pepper

Bring the stock to the boil and add a little extra salt before putting in the rice. Boil for just under 15 minutes until the rice is tender but not getting soggy. While this is cooking, beat the egg in a bowl, beat in the lemon juice and then very slowly add a little of the hot soup. If this operation is done too quickly it will spoil the texture of the soup. Pour the egg and lemon sauce into the soup and stir gently. Season with salt and pepper and reheat. Stand a couple of minutes off the heat before serving.

Beef goulash soup

This soup is very warming and nourishing and, as those who are skiers will know, is often served on the ski slopes. It is tastier prepared in advance and reheated.

Cooking time 1-1½ hours Working time 15-20 minutes

1 large onion	several tomatoes
25 g (1 oz) butter	½ litre (1 pint) water
¼ kg (½ lb) beef	2 large potatoes
1 heaped teaspoon paprika	salt

Chop the onion and sauté in the butter. Meanwhile, cut the meat into small pieces. Remove the onions from the heat and stir in the paprika. Add the meat and fry gently for a further 5 minutes. Skin the tomatoes by immersing in boiling water for a minute, then chop them. Add the tomatoes and most of the water to the meat; season, cover and cook slowly for 1 hour or until the meat is tender. Peel and dice the potatoes and add to the soup with the rest of the water. Continue cooking until the potatoes are tender.

Serving suggestion: Serve with hunks of fresh bread.

Chicken and almond soup

An interesting variation on the usual chicken soup.

Cooking time 1 hour 5 minutes-1 hour 20 minutes
Working time 15-20 minutes

2 tablespoons olive oil
1 chicken leg
½ litre (1 pint) water
½ small onion, chopped
1 clove garlic, crushed

75-100 g (3-4 oz) ground *or* very
　finely chopped almonds
1 tablespoon chopped parsley
15 g (½ oz) breadcrumbs
salt and pepper

Heat 1 tablespoon of the oil in a saucepan, put in the chicken leg and sauté until it is browned on all sides. Add the water, bring to the boil, lower the heat, cover and simmer for 20-30 minutes until the meat will come easily from the bone. Reserve the stock. Heat the remainder of the oil in a pan and sauté the chopped onion, crushed garlic, almonds and half the parsley until the onions are transparent. Add the breadcrumbs and cook for a further 2-3 minutes, then add the stock and the chicken meat. Season with salt and pepper. Cover the pan and cook for a further 30 minutes. Garnish with the remainder of the parsley.

Cheese soup

Cooking time 20 minutes Working time 20 minutes

50 g (2 oz) butter
1 onion, finely chopped
1 stick celery, finely chopped
1 clove garlic, crushed
1 tablespoon flour
¼ kg (½ lb) mature Cheddar cheese

½ litre (1 pint) milk
1 glass white wine (optional)
salt and pepper
pinch of cayenne pepper
dash of Tabasco sauce (optional)

Melt the butter in a saucepan, add the chopped onions and celery, the crushed garlic and sauté until softened. Blend in the flour, lower the heat and add the cheese, milk and wine, stirring continuously with a wooden spoon. Season with salt and pepper and a little cayenne pepper. A dash of Tabasco sauce can also be added, particularly if you are not using the wine. Continue cooking over a low heat for 10 minutes, stirring occasionally until the floury flavour has gone.

Serving suggestion: Cut some bread into small cubes and fry in butter or lard. Scatter these on to the soup.

Gazpacho

This is a traditional Andalucian summer soup which is now popular all over Spain. We used to make it (when we had a spare hour or so!) by hand, which is the way it always used to be made. However, this is really very time-consuming and for this reason most Spanish housewives now use an electric blender. Gazpacho made this way is, to my mind, inferior to that made by hand, but it depends on the time you have to spend and, of course, whether or not you have a blender. (We didn't, hence the puritanical approach!)

Serves 4 Cooking time none Working time – by hand 1 hour – by blender 20-30 minutes

2 tablespoons breadcrumbs	2 cloves garlic
1½-2 tablespoons wine vinegar	2 tablespoons olive oil
¾ kg (1½ lb) tomatoes	water
½ cucumber, peeled	salt
1 green pepper	red pepper (optional)
1 onion	

Soak the breadcrumbs in the vinegar. Skin the tomatoes by immersing them in boiling water for a minute. Chop the tomatoes, cucumber, green pepper and onion. If using a blender, put in all the ingredients except the water. When the mixture is blended add water until the desired consistency is reached. As in many Spanish recipes, this seemed to be a question of personal taste. I have been served both very thick and quite thin gazpacho.

If you are not using a blender, chop up the ingredients as finely as possible and pound well with the soaked breadcrumbs. Pass through a vegetable mill, using the water to help get them through. Add the oil and mix well. Season with salt and, if desired, a little red pepper. Extra vinegar, or oil, can be added at this stage if wished. Add a few ice cubes and serve well chilled.

Gazpacho is often garnished with finely chopped tomato, green pepper, onion, cucumber, and hardboiled egg, each served in a separate small dish. This is not really necessary if the gazpacho is made by hand, as the individual vegetables are distinguishable and the consistency 'rough', but if done in the blender the garnishes definitely add the finishing touch.

Chilled cucumber soup

This is a delicious soup for a summer evening which can be easily prepared and left in the fridge until required. The cream is added just before serving.

Cooking time 20 minutes Working time 10 minutes

½ litre (1 pint) boiling water
2 chicken stock cubes
1 small onion
1 large cucumber

sprig of mint
salt and pepper
1 dessertspoon cornflour (optional)
small tub of single cream

Pour the boiling water on to the stock cubes and mix well. Slice the onion finely. Peel and chop the cucumber (saving a little for garnish). Put the onion and cucumber into a saucepan with the stock and a couple of mint leaves. Bring to the boil, lower the heat, cover and simmer gently for 15-20 minutes. Blend in a liquidiser or pass through a fine sieve. Season with salt and pepper, remembering that the stock cubes are already salty. At this stage if you wish to make a thicker soup, a dessertspoon of cornflour may be mixed with cold water and blended with the contents of the saucepan. Cook for a further 5 minutes if doing this, otherwise simply leave the soup in the refrigerator to chill and stir in the cream just before serving. Garnish with slices of cucumber and the rest of the mint, chopped.

2 Eggs

Eggs are an absolutely basic 'must' for the larder at all times. I think most people will agree that they are one of the most versatile ingredients we have in cooking. Before going on to give some useful recipes for impromptu lunch or supper dishes, I felt it might be helpful just to recap on the basic ways of cooking eggs. Who needs an oven when you have eggs!

Boiled eggs

Surprising how often people are unable to get these to turn out as they want them! There are several different preferred methods of dealing with them. Plunging the eggs into boiling water and boiling for $3\frac{1}{2}$-$4\frac{1}{2}$ minutes according to taste seems to be the most popular method, although many complain that the eggs often crack this way. This is less likely to happen if the eggs are not kept in the fridge. If it does then a little salt added to the water solidifies the white and stops it from disappearing in trails into the water. Hardboiled eggs need about 10 minutes and should then be plunged into cold water; this prevents grey rings forming around the edge of the yolks.

Coddled eggs

Essentially the same as boiling, it is a method which produces rather softer, creamier whites than the usual methods. Put the eggs into boiling water for 1 minute only, then remove the pan from the heat and time the eggs from then for 5 minutes.

Poached eggs

Fill a wide pan two-thirds full of water, add a pinch of salt and a teaspoon of vinegar (wine vinegar preferably). Bring to the boil, break each egg into a cup, slide into the water and simmer for 2-3 minutes until firm. Take out with a draining spoon. Swirling the water round and slipping the egg into the centre helps get the white around the yolk. Poached eggs can be kept warm by putting immediately into a bowl of hand-hot water, or alternatively may be reheated if put immediately into cold water and later adding enough boiling water to bring the temperature up to hand-hot. This is useful should you, for example, wish to serve them with a sauce, such as a cheese sauce.

To my mind this traditional way of poaching eggs is far preferable to doing them in a poaching pan, where the eggs are in fact steamed rather than poached.

Fried eggs

Many people use lard in which to fry eggs, but I must confess that my more extravagant preference is for either butter, or a mixture of butter and olive oil. As long as you have a reasonable pan, 25 g (1 oz) of butter and 1 teaspoon of oil should be sufficient for a couple of eggs. You might need more if using a large pan. Heat the butter and oil until the butter has melted and is beginning to bubble slightly. Slide in the eggs and cook for 2-3 minutes. They may be quickly flipped over to set the white on top of the yolk.

Scrambled eggs

This is yet another way of cooking with eggs where most people have their well-defined preferences. Some like more butter, others more milk, some like them very creamy, others prefer the end result to be more solid. However, as a basis from which to work out your own preferences I would suggest that to two eggs (for 1 person) you take about 20 g ($\frac{3}{4}$ oz) butter and between 1 and 2 tablespoons of milk or cream. Beat the eggs well with a fork, add the milk and salt and pepper to taste. Melt the butter in a saucepan, pour in the eggs and cook gently over a low to moderate heat, stirring with a wooden spoon, until the eggs begin to set. Continue stirring until they have reached the desired consistency, not forgetting that they will continue to cook from the heat of the pan.

Omelette

A lot of mystique seems to surround the making of a good French omelette, which to my mind is actually a simpler operation than trying to get a boiled egg the consistency you want it. At least you can see what is happening when you are cooking an omelette. Boiled eggs seem to depend on factors like the size of the egg and things that nowadays you can rarely know, like how fresh the eggs are. A good omelette will also depend on how fresh the eggs are, but at least you have a little more control over the consistency it attains.

As with the fried eggs, I tend to use a little olive oil as well as butter for omelettes, about 15-20 g ($\frac{1}{2}$-$\frac{3}{4}$ oz) butter to 1 teaspoon oil and 2-3 eggs. I do not add water to the egg as it seems to have a detrimental effect on the consistency of the omelette. Beat the eggs in a bowl, just enough to break the yolk into the white. Literally a few turns of the fork is almost sufficient. Season with salt and pepper. Heat the pan thoroughly before adding the oil and butter. Almost immediately add the egg mixture, giving it a few swirls with the flat of a fork. This gets some of the raw egg on to the hot pan. The bottom of the omelette will be set within a matter of seconds and after the initial swirling with the fork, move the pan around gently whilst loosening the sides of the omelette so that more of the uncooked mixture will run down on to the bottom of the pan. The whole process should take no more than a couple of minutes, if that, and the top of the omelette (the part which becomes the middle as you roll it out on to the plate) should remain soft and slightly runny. Preheated fillings may be added halfway through the cooking process or if you are not sufficiently confident to do this, simply spoon over the top of the omelette before serving. Alternatively, chopped ham or fresh herbs may be added to the egg mixture.

Bacon omelette

2-4 rashers bacon	1 teaspoon olive oil
4 eggs	25-30 g (1 oz) butter
salt and pepper	

Dice the bacon. Prepare the eggs as above. Fry the bacon pieces gently in the oil and half the butter. Add the remainder of the butter, turn up the heat and add the egg mixture. Finish as above.

Mushroom omelette

50-100 g (2-4 oz) mushrooms	4 eggs
50 g (2 oz) butter	salt and pepper

Prepare the eggs as above. Clean the mushrooms gently with a damp cloth. It is not necessary to peel them unless they are very old. Slice thinly and fry very gently in half the butter in an omelette pan. Add the remainder of the butter, pour in the egg mixture and proceed as above.

Note: In both the above recipes it is probably better to perform the operation twice as it is harder to get the omelette to the right consistency with too many eggs in the pan.

Omelette fillings
Tomato and green pepper

Cooking time 20 minutes Working time 10 minutes

6-7 tomatoes	olive oil
1 small onion	salt and pepper
½-1 green pepper	1 tablespoon tomato pureé

Skin the tomatoes by first immersing them in boiling water for a minute, then chop them. Slice the onion and green pepper finely and fry in a little olive oil until soft. Add the tomatoes and season with salt and pepper. Cover and cook for 10 minutes. Add the tomato pureé and cook for a further 5 minutes. Put half this mixture in the centre of each omelette before folding out on to the plates, or alternatively spread over the top.

Tuna fish with mushroom and soured cream

Working time 5 minutes

a few raw mushrooms	salt and pepper
1 small tin tuna fish	1-2 tablespoons soured cream
lemon juice	

Slice the mushrooms finely. Mix all the ingredients together and put into the centre of the omelette just before serving. The mixture may be heated in a saucepan first.

Other suggestions for omelettes

Make an omelette *aux fines herbes* and put into the actual egg mixture any fresh or dried herbs you like and have available. Fresh parsley is, of course, the obvious one; tarragon, oregano and thyme you will probably have dried if not fresh.

Add diced ham, or if the budget runs to it, pieces of smoked salmon are delicious (also very good in scrambled eggs). Grated cheese may be put into the egg mixture or sprinkled on top.

Tortilla Espanola

Cooking time 20 minutes Working time 20 minutes
+ 15 minutes

oil	4 eggs
1 large potato	salt and pepper
1 small onion	chopped parsley
2 cloves garlic	

In a small, deep, thick-bottomed frying pan heat enough oil to deep-fry the potato. Peel and cut the potato into small cubes (less than 1 cm, ½ in) and fry. Chop the onion and garlic finely and add to the pan after a few minutes, so that they finish cooking at the same time as the potato.

Meanwhile, break the eggs into a bowl, season with salt and pepper, add a little chopped parsley to taste and beat well.

When the potato, onion and garlic are fried, remove from the oil with a draining spoon, put them into the egg mixture and leave them to stand for 15 minutes. Pour as much oil as possible out of the frying pan, leaving only a thin film on the bottom. Pour the egg mixture into the pan and cook, without stirring, on the lowest possible heat. When the outside edges are cooked, cover the pan with a plate, turn it upside down and then slide the omelette back into the pan so that the cooked side is now on top. The consistency of the uncooked part at this point will depend on the amount of oil, the quantity of potatoes and onions, and the heat at which it has been cooked. If it is too liquid, the turning operation may prove rather hazardous! To avoid this, pour out the liquid on to another plate before inverting the pan, and pour it back before sliding the cooked part on top. This is not considered by the Spaniards to be correct technique, but is often unavoidable. After a few minutes the other side is cooked and the centre should be slightly less solid than the surface.

Serving suggestion: The omelette may be eaten hot but is generally served cold. It is an excellent dish for a buffet supper or lunch and can also be cut into small portions to be eaten as *tapas* with pre-meal drinks.

Note: This omelette is not like a French omelette, and much of its success depends on slow cooking.

Fried eggs with tomatoes and peppers

Cooking time 25 minutes Working time 10 minutes

1 red *or* green pepper	1 clove garlic
olive oil and butter	salt and pepper
¼ kg (½ lb) tomatoes	4 eggs

Wash the pepper, remove the stalk end and the pips and cut into slices. Fry gently in a little olive oil in a covered pan for 10 minutes. Meanwhile, skin and cut up the tomatoes and chop the garlic. After the 10 minutes add the tomatoes and garlic to the peppers. Season with salt and pepper and cook for a further 10 minutes until the tomato is well blended.

Fry the eggs in a mixture of oil and butter and serve with the vegetables. Don't forget the bread for mopping up!

Frothy eggs

Cooking time 10 minutes Working time 10 minutes

¼ kg (½ lb) tomatoes	50 g (2 oz) butter
4 eggs	salt and pepper

Skin and cut up the tomatoes. Separate the eggs and beat the yolks. Whisk the egg whites until they are stiff enough to stand in peaks. Melt the butter in a pan and add the tomatoes, seasoning well with salt and pepper. Cook, covered, until they have formed a pureé. At this stage add the yolks and stir quickly so that they are thoroughly blended with the pureé. Before they are set, add the whites and whisk well. Serve at once.

Piperade

This is not in fact a truly Basque *piperade*, which requires more tomatoes and peppers to the quantity of eggs but it is a very good light supper or lunch dish served with bacon or ham or simply with brown bread and butter.

Cooking time 20-25 minutes Working time 10-15 minutes

½ onion	1 dessertspoon oil
3-4 tomatoes	salt and pepper
2 green peppers	4 eggs, beaten

Slice the onion finely. Skin the tomatoes and slice the green peppers. Fry the onions and peppers gently in the oil until softened, about 10 minutes. Add the tomatoes and season with salt and pepper. Cover and cook until a purée is formed. Add the beaten eggs and stir until they begin to thicken. Remove from the heat and allow to finish cooking by the heat of the pan. Serve immediately.

Brunch special

Cooking time 35 minutes Working time 35 minutes

2 large potatoes	1 large onion
4-6 sausages	knob of butter
knob of lard	salt and pepper
1 cooking apple	3-4 eggs

Boil the potatoes in their skins until soft when tested with a fork. Remove the skins. This is in fact done most easily when the potatoes are still hot. Slice them thinly. Fry the sausages in a little lard, then drain and slice. Peel and core the cooking apple. Slice the onion and apple and fry gently in the butter. Add the potatoes and sausages, season with salt and pepper and heat through. Hollow out a space for the eggs and break them on top of the mixture in the pan. Cover and cook over a very low heat until the eggs are set.

Note: This dish is best cooked in a pan that can be brought straight to the table.

Stuffed eggs

Cooking time 10 minutes Working time 10-15 minutes

4 eggs	1 teaspoon lemon juice
3 dessertspoons tuna fish *or*	salt
cooked and peeled prawns	1 lettuce, finely chopped
4 green olives, chopped	3 dessertspoons mayonnaise
1 small tinned red pepper, chopped	

Hardboil the eggs. Plunge into cold water and remove the shells. Cut them in half lengthwise. Remove the yolks and reserve. Mix together the tuna or prawns (cut small), the chopped olives and red pepper (reserving a little of each for decoration), the lemon juice and salt. Fill the egg halves with this mixture and arrange on a plate on a bed of finely chopped lettuce. Sprinkle with the egg yolks and spoon over the mayonnaise. Garnish with the chopped olives and red pepper.

Eggs avocado

A delicious summer lunch!

Cooking time 10 minutes Working time 10-15 minutes

4 eggs
1 tablespoon natural yogurt
¼ teaspoon finely grated lemon
  rind
dash of Tabasco sauce
salt and pepper

1 avocado
4 tomatoes
2 sticks celery
1 lettuce
parsley

Hardboil the eggs. Plunge into cold water and remove the shells. Slice them in half lengthwise. Remove the yolks and mash them well, then add the yogurt, grated lemon rind, Tabasco sauce, salt and pepper. Peel, stone and mash the avocado, mix with the egg mixture, and use to fill the egg halves.

Slice the tomatoes and chop the celery and arrange on a bed of lettuce. Place the eggs on top and garnish with fresh parsley.

Serving suggestion: Serve with brown bread and butter or crispbread.

Curried eggs

Cooking time 10 minutes Working time 5 minutes

4 eggs
a little curry powder
a good teaspoon mayonnaise

salt and pepper
watercress

Put the eggs into a pan and cover with cold water. Bring to the boil and cook for 7-10 minutes. Drain off the hot water and run plenty of cold water over them. Shell and slice lengthwise. Scoop out the yolks into a small bowl, add curry powder to taste (the mild kind is best for this), mayonnaise, salt and pepper and mix well together. Press this mixture back into the egg halves and arrange them on a bed of watercress.

Serving suggestion: Serve with thinly sliced brown bread and butter.

Oeufs en cocotte

This is a very simple light dish which seems traditionally to be made in the oven. However, it can be cooked equally well on top. If this is being served as a main course, open egg dishes serve the purpose rather better than *cocotte* dishes, which can really hold only one egg. In its simplest form this dish comprises nothing more than egg and cream, but the version below adds a bit of extra interest to the basic recipe. Any of the omelette fillings given on pages 36-7 can equally well be put into the bottom of the dishes.

Cooking time 10 minutes Working time 10 minutes

25 g (1 oz) mushrooms	4 eggs
25 g (1 oz) cooked ham	2 tablespoons double cream
25 g (1 oz) butter	salt and pepper

Chop the mushrooms very finely and dice the ham. Butter the cocottes or egg dishes and break two eggs into each, then sprinkle the ham and mushrooms into the dishes. Pour a tablespoon of cream over each, season with salt and pepper and dot with the remaining butter. Put the dishes into a baking dish and pour into the baking dish enough hot water to come halfway up the sides of the cocottes. Cook for 8-10 minutes until the eggs are lightly set.

Serving suggestion: Serve with bread and butter.

3 Beef, veal and liver

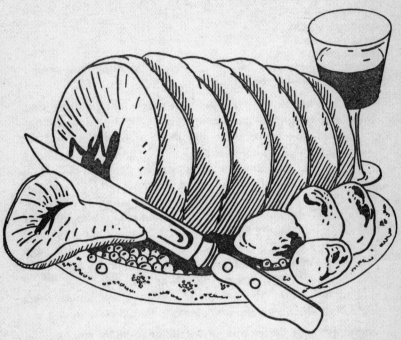

Most of the recipes in this chapter are for beef. I have included a number of recipes for composite dishes which are very useful when cooking on the top, particularly in circumstances where facilities really are limited. Dishes such as the Super Stew (see page 46) and the Beef 'n' Brown Ale (see page 44) are also ideal for improvisation – don't worry if you haven't got exactly what the recipe says; perhaps you've got something else that will add a different flavour? The remaining recipes are for veal and liver although veal can, of course, always be cooked in any of the ways suggested for beef. It is also very well suited to the recipes for pork fillets in Chapter 4.

Spicy estofada

Cooking time 1¾ hours + 1 hour marinating
Working time 30 minutes

¼ kg (½ lb) braising steak
2 glasses wine
sunflower *or* olive oil
½ cinnamon stick
freshly grated nutmeg
crushed peppercorns
1 small clove garlic, crushed

1 stick celery
1 onion
12 almonds, grated
stock
salt
100 g (4 oz) mushrooms, sliced

Cut the meat into cubes. Make up a marinade of 1 glass wine, 1 tablespoon oil, the cinnamon stick, a little grated nutmeg, several crushed peppercorns and the crushed garlic. Add the meat and marinate for 1 hour.

Chop the celery, slice the onion and fry gently in a little oil until the onion is soft. Remove and put aside. In the same pan brown the drained meat adding a little extra oil if necessary. Return the vegetables to the pan, add the grated almonds, any marinade that hasn't been soaked up by the meat (removing the cinnamon stick), the remaining glass of wine and enough stock to cover the meat. Bring to the boil, lower the heat, cover and cook gently for 1 hour. Add salt at this stage and continue cooking for another 15 minutes, then add the sliced mushrooms and adjust the seasoning. Cook for a further 10-15 minutes.

Serving suggestion: Serve with tagliatelle or plain boiled rice.

Beef 'n' brown ale

Cooking time 1½ hours Working time 20 minutes

knob of butter
1 tablespoon oil
1 large onion, sliced
¼ kg (½ lb) minced beef
1 can brown ale
1 large carrot, sliced

1 small green pepper, sliced
1 tablespoon tomato pureé
1 bayleaf
1 teaspoon paprika
salt and pepper
100 g (4 oz) mushrooms, sliced

Melt the butter and the oil in a pan. Fry the sliced onion until softened, remove and brown the meat. Pour in the brown ale and add the onions, sliced carrot, half the sliced green pepper, the tomato pureé, bayleaf and paprika. Season with salt and pepper. Cover and cook for 1 hour, then add the sliced mushrooms and the rest of the green pepper. Cook for a further 15 minutes.

Serving suggestion: This goes well with pureéd potatoes (see page 130).

Beef and olive casserole

Cooking time 1½-2 hours + 2 hours marinating
Working time 30 minutes

For the marinade:

1 small carrot	¼ kg (½ lb) braising or rump steak
1 small onion	oil
1 stick celery	2 rashers fat bacon
1½ tablespoons olive oil	2 rashers lean bacon
1 glass red wine	1 glass red wine
½ glass wine vinegar	green and black olives
a small bunch of fresh herbs	2-3 tomatoes
(thyme, parsley, etc)	
1 clove garlic	
a few crushed black peppercorns	

To prepare the marinade, dice the vegetables. Heat the oil in a small saucepan, add the vegetables and fry until lightly browned. Add the other ingredients and simmer gently for 10 minutes. While it is cooling, cut the meat into chunks, lay it in a porcelain dish and pour the marinade over. Leave for 2 hours.

Cut the bacon into small pieces. Remove the meat from the marinade and drain, reserving the marinade. Put a little oil into the pan and brown the bacon and meat. Add the marinade, wine and olives and if necessary a little stock or water. Cover with greased greaseproof paper, then cover with a lid and cook gently for 1½-2 hours or until the meat is tender.

Skin and chop the tomatoes and add to the casserole 15 minutes before serving.

Serving suggestion: Serve with green tagliatelle.

Beef and mushroom casserole with soured cream

Cooking time 2 hours Working time 35 minutes

¼ kg (½ lb) braising steak	water
1 medium onion	salt and pepper
1-2 tablespoons olive oil	sprinkling hot red pepper
knob of butter	½ teaspoon mustard
3 tomatoes	1 slice lemon
1 dessertspoon flour	150 g (6 oz) mushrooms, sliced
	½ small carton soured cream

Cut the steak into small pieces. Slice the onion. Put half the oil into the pan with the butter. Brown the meat, remove and put aside on a plate. Add the remainder of the olive oil to the pan and fry the onions until soft. While they are frying, peel and chop the tomatoes. Add the tomatoes and the meat to the onions and fry for 3-5 minutes, then sprinkle with the flour and cover with water. Put in the salt, pepper, red pepper, mustard and slice of lemon. Bring to the boil, lower the heat, cover and cook for 1½-2 hours or until the meat is tender. In the last 15-20 minutes of cooking add the sliced mushrooms. Just before serving, stir in the soured cream.

Serving suggestion: Serve on a bed of rice or with noodles.

Super stew

Cooking time 2 hours Working time 25-35 minutes

¼ kg (½ lb) stewing/braising steak	1 onion, sliced
olive oil	1 large carrot, sliced

1 green pepper, sliced
3 tomatoes, peeled and chopped
1 clove garlic, chopped
red wine
water

1 tablespoon concentrated tomato purée
bouquet garni
salt and pepper
1 large potato, peeled and diced

Cut the meat into good-sized pieces. Heat enough oil to just cover the bottom of your saucepan. Brown the meat in the oil, remove and then soften the sliced onion. Add the sliced carrot, half the sliced green pepper, the peeled and chopped tomatoes and the chopped garlic. With the lid on, fry all these ingredients gently for a further 5-10 minutes. After this time, add equal quantities of red wine and water to cover the ingredients. Add the tomato purée and bouquet garni and season with salt and pepper. Cover and cook gently for 1½-2 hours, adding the peeled and diced potato about halfway through. 15 minutes before the stew is finished, add the remaining slices of green pepper. This adds a fresh flavour and colour to the finished stew.

Note: This is a meal in itself – hence the name!

Goulash

This dish was a favourite of my grandmother who learnt it from her husband, a Hungarian. The most important ingredient is the red pepper (paprika), which must be the Hungarian type. The Spanish pepper has a different flavour.

Cooking time 2 hours Working time 25 minutes

1-2 dessertspoons of oil or a knob of lard
1 onion, sliced
¼ kg (½ lb) chuck steak
salt
Hungarian paprika
2 tablespoons tomato purée

cumin seeds
stock
1 large green pepper, sliced
knob of butter
soured cream (optional)
caraway seeds (optional)

Heat the oil or lard in a casserole and soften the sliced onion without browning it. Cut the meat into pieces and add to the pan. Cook until browned, then season with salt and paprika. The amount of paprika used depends totally on the quality and strength. Whether the paprika is hot or mild depends on the region from which it comes. The best comes from Szeged in the south and is mild, but which you use is a question of preference. Add the tomato purée, a few cumin and caraway seeds and just enough stock to cover. Put on the lid of the casserole and stew gently for 1½-2 hours, adding the sliced green pepper 15-20 minutes before the end. The characteristic colour of goulash is obtained by adding the following mixture just before serving: in a small pan melt a very small knob of butter, stir in quickly a little Hungarian paprika and immediately add a little warm water. Soured cream may be added just before serving.

Beef and leeks in red wine

Cooking time 1½ hours Working time 15-20 minutes

2 large leeks	2 glasses red wine
¼ kg (½ lb) braising steak	2-3 glasses water *or* stock
25 g (1 oz) butter	2-3 pinches of cumin seed
1 tablespoon olive oil	salt and pepper

Wash the leeks thoroughly. This is best done by cutting off the 'tatty' dark green parts of the leaves (usually down to about 2 cm (1 in) above the white part) and making two deep cuts which cross each other. This enables you to splay the leaves and remove any lodged particles of mud or grit under running water.

Cut the meat into cubes. Once they are cleaned, slice the leeks and sauté in the butter. Remove from the pan, add the olive oil and brown the meat. Add the wine, stock, cumin, salt and pepper. Cover and cook very gently for 1-1½ hours, returning the leeks to the pan about 20 minutes before the dish is to be served.

Serving suggestion: Serve with tagliatelle or boiled potatoes and salad.

Steak with cream and mushrooms

Cooking time 10 minutes Working time 10 minutes

100 g (4 oz) mushrooms	freshly milled *or* crushed black
olive oil and butter	peppercorns
2 fillet or rump steaks	1 dessertspoon brandy (optional)
1 clove garlic	3-4 tablespoons cream

Slice the mushrooms finely and sauté gently in butter for about 5 minutes. Remove and put aside on a plate. Rub the steaks with the clove of garlic and sprinkle over some black pepper to taste. Add a little olive oil to the pan, turn up the heat and fry the steaks according to your preference. For a rare steak, a minute on each side is sufficient, even less if it is thin. Remove and put with the mushrooms. Add the brandy, allow to bubble well for a few moments, then add the cream and the mushrooms, bring to simmering point before adding the steak just to warm it through.

Serving suggestion: Serve with French fried potatoes (see page 129) and salad.

Beef curry

Cooking time 2 hours Working time 25 minutes

¼ kg (½ lb) chuck steak	1 carrot, sliced
2 tablespoons olive oil	handful of raisins
1 small onion, sliced	handful of unsalted peanuts
1 small apple, chopped	extra ground ginger
1 tablespoon curry powder	*or* ginger root
½ tablespoon flour	extra turmeric
½ litre (¾ pint) stock	1 chilli pepper, sliced
1 tomato, peeled and chopped	1 slice of lemon
(optional)	squeeze of lemon juice
1 clove garlic, chopped	desiccated coconut

Cut the meat into cubes and brown in the oil. Remove and fry the sliced onion in the pan until softened. Add the chopped apple and sprinkle over the curry powder and the flour. Fry for 2 minutes, then add the stock, the peeled and chopped tomato, the chopped garlic, the sliced carrot, the raisins, peanuts, a sprinkling of extra ginger and turmeric, the sliced chilli pepper and the slice of lemon cut into small pieces. Cover and cook for 1½-2 hours and just before serving add a squeeze of lemon juice. Put a dish of desiccated coconut on the table to sprinkle over the curry.

Serving suggestion: Serve with plain boiled or saffron rice (see page 108).

Homemade burgers

Cooking time 35 minutes Working time 35 minutes

1 medium carrot	chopped parsley
1 medium onion	salt and pepper
½ small green pepper	1 level tablespoon fresh brown
¼ kg (½ lb) minced beef	breadcrumbs
50 g (2 oz) sausage meat	oil
1 egg, beaten	

Chop the carrot and cook until soft in a little boiling salted water. Drain off the water and mash the carrot. Put aside. Meanwhile, dice the onion and green pepper finely and fry gently until soft in a little oil. While this mixture is frying, stir together in a bowl the minced beef, sausage meat and the beaten egg. Add chopped parsley to taste and the mashed carrot. Season with salt and pepper; about ½ teaspoon of salt should be enough. When the onion and green pepper are cooked, add them to the meat mixture with the breadcrumbs.

The mixture should now be divided and dropped in very large spoonfuls on to a plate of flour. These quantities of ingredients should make about four 'burgers'. Once floured the burgers can be shaped and should ideally be as flat as possible as this makes them easier to cook through. It is very easy if one is not careful to end up with things that look well done on the outside, but which turn out to be still raw inside! The burgers should be shallow-fried in hot fat for about 15 minutes, taking care not to cook them too quickly to start with, although making sure, of course, that the fat is hot enough when they are first put in – otherwise they will be greasy.

Serving suggestion: Serve with your favourite vegetable.

Albondigas
Spanish meatballs

Cooking time 1½ hours Working time 50 minutes

¼ kg (½ lb) minced pork	flour
1 dessertspoon oregano	½ onion
1 bunch parsley, chopped	lard, butter *or* oil
1 egg	¼ kg (½ lb) potatoes
salt and pepper	5 tomatoes
	water

In a bowl mix together the minced pork, the oregano and the chopped parsley. Beat the egg well and stir into the pork mixture. Season with salt and pepper. Put a little flour into a cup then put in a little lump of meat mixture and shake around until it forms a flour-coated ball. Repeat until all the meat is used.

Slice the onion and fry gently in the fat or oil. Add the albondigas and cook slowly, making sure that they don't fall to pieces. They should take 30-40 minutes.

While they are cooking, peel the potatoes and cut these into slices. Peel and chop the tomatoes. When the albondigas are ready take them out of the pan and put them aside on a plate. Fry the slices of potato in the fat in the pan for 10 minutes, then add the tomatoes. Cook for a further 5 minutes and add some water. Stir well, making sure that all the grease is amalgamated with the liquid. Season this sauce with salt and pepper. Bring to the boil, lower the heat, cover and simmer until the potatoes are cooked. Add the albondigas just before the end to heat through.

Serving suggestion: A very good vegetable to go with this dish is peas, which can be added to the sauce and cooked in the same pan.

Veal in mustard and caper sauce

Cooking time 40-50 minutes Working time 40 minutes

2 rashers streaky bacon
1 tablespoon oil
2 veal cutlets
20 g (¾ oz) butter
20 g (¾ oz) flour

2 teaspoons dry mustard
¼ litre (½ pint) milk
salt and pepper
1 tablespoon drained capers

Dice the bacon and fry gently in the oil for 5 minutes. Turn up the heat, and add the veal cutlets to the pan. Seal these quickly on both sides, then lower the heat and cook for a further 5 minutes on each side. Remove the cutlets and bacon and put aside whilst preparing the sauce in the same pan. Melt the butter, then stir in the flour, mustard and milk. Season with salt and pepper. Continue to stir gently with a wooden spoon until the sauce thickens, then add the capers and return the meat to the pan. Simmer gently for 5-10 minutes.

Serving suggestion: Serve with sauté potatoes (see page 130).

Note: If you want to make this dish more exotic, use cream instead of making the white sauce.

Veal with orange

Cooking time ¾ hour Working time 5-10 minutes

½ onion
knob of butter
2-4 veal fillets
½ clove garlic
juice of 1 orange

1 bayleaf
pinch of cinnamon
salt and pepper
water
2 slices of orange

Slice the onion finely and sauté gently until soft in a little butter. Remove, add a little extra butter to the pan and brown the veal fillets with the ½ clove of garlic. Remove the garlic clove and add the orange juice, bay leaf and cinnamon. Cover and simmer over a very low heat for 15-20 minutes, then add a little water. Continue to cook gently until the veal is tender. Serve garnished with the slices of orange.

Serving suggestion: Buttered noodles go well with this dish.

Breaded veal cutlets

Cooking time 15-20 minutes Working time 20-25 minutes

2-3 tablespoons flour	1 egg
½ teaspoon salt	1 tablespoon water
½ teaspoon paprika	50 g (2 oz) breadcrumbs
freshly milled pepper	oil *or* lard
2 veal cutlets	

Mix together the flour, salt, paprika and pepper. Coat the meat with this mixture. (A good way of doing this is in a plastic bag.) Break the egg into a basin and beat lightly with the water. Dip the cutlets into the egg and coat with the breadcrumbs. Heat the oil or lard in a frying pan and fry the breaded cutlets until golden.

Serving suggestion: This is very good served with the barbecue sauce on page 67.

Liver casserole

Cooking time 45 minutes Working time 20-25 minutes

½ onion	peppercorns
2 carrots	salt
1 rasher streaky bacon	100 g (4 oz) mushrooms
¼ kg (½ lb) calf's *or* pig's liver	bouquet garni
butter and lard	chicken stock
1 small clove garlic	

Chop the onion and slice the carrots thinly. Remove the rind from the bacon. Cut the bacon and the liver into small pieces. In a casserole gently soften the onion and carrot in butter. Crush several peppercorns in a pestle and mortar or roughly grind in a mill. Sprinkle these over the vegetables. Season with salt. Once the carrot and onion are well softened (10-15 minutes), melt a little lard and butter in a frying pan. In this fry the bacon for 1 minute, then add the pieces of liver and fry for a further 2 minutes to seal them. Tip these into the casserole with the carrot and onion and add the mushrooms, bouquet garni, garlic clove and enough stock to cover. Cover and cook for 30 minutes.

Serving suggestions: Mashed potatoes make a good accompaniment.

Hungarian liver casserole

Cooking time 35 minutes Working time 10 minutes

½ onion	brown stock
½ green pepper	1 tablespoon soured cream
¼ kg (½ lb) calf's *or* pig's liver	salt and pepper
lard	paprika

Slice the onion and green pepper and cut the liver into small pieces. Fry these together in a little lard, stirring to make sure they don't stick. Add a small amount of brown stock, cover and cook gently for 30 minutes. Just before serving, thicken the gravy with the soured cream and season to taste with salt, pepper and paprika.

Serving suggestion: Serve with a version of the Patatas Riojana on page 131 made without wine.

Liver in red wine

Cooking time 20-25 minutes Working time 15 minutes

1 large onion
butter and olive oil
½ teaspoon crushed black
  peppercorns

¼ kg (½ lb) calf's *or* pig's liver
1 glass of red wine

Slice the onion into rings and fry gently until soft in a little butter and oil with the crushed peppercorns. If the liver is cut 'lumpily', try and slice it into thin fillets with a sharp knife. This way it can be cooked quickly and does not become tough. Fry the liver in the pan with the onions for 5-10 minutes, then add the wine and cook for a further 5-10 minutes.

Serving suggestion: Serve with boiled or mashed potatoes.

Liver creole

Cooking time 30 minutes Working time 15 minutes

1 green pepper
2 rashers bacon
¼ kg (½ lb) calf's liver
flour
1 teaspoon oil

1 small tin tomatoes
salt
chilli powder
cayenne pepper

Slice the green pepper into strips. Fry the bacon until crisp, then remove from the pan. Cut the liver into strips about 2 cm (1 in) wide and coat in flour. This is best done by putting 2-3 tablespoons of flour into a plastic bag, dropping the pieces of liver in and shaking until they are coated. Shake the excess flour from the liver and brown in the bacon fat and the oil. Add the green pepper and the tinned tomatoes. Season to taste. Go carefully with the chilli powder and the cayenne pepper! Less than ½ a teaspoon of the former should be about right and a pinch of the latter. Cover the pan and cook gently for 15 minutes. Return the bacon to the pan a couple of minutes before the end just to warm it through.

4 Lamb and pork

In England lamb is a popular meat which more often than not tends to be roasted. This chapter suggests some alternative ways of cooking it. Don't be afraid to use a good cut of meat for a casserole – it can only improve the casserole and it won't spoil the meat! Buying a small leg of lamb for two people is not an extravagance; what you don't use can be put into a bean, rice or pasta dish the following day.

Pork was one of my favourite meats when I was living in Spain – it was quite honestly so much tastier than the meat one usually comes across here. However, I hope that some of these recipes will help make even the most tasteless piece of meat into something interesting.

Amongst the recipes in this chapter are some for sausages, although one or two appear elsewhere in the book. Sausages of all kinds can be used to make some very good dishes. They team very well with beans (see page 102), and the Spanish sausage, chorizo, a highly flavoured spicy red sausage, which turns up in various forms and can be bought here in delicatessens, adds a very interesting flavour to anything it is cooked with. Recipes using this appear on pages 104, 105-6 and 112. The recipes in this chapter use ordinary 'bangers', frankfurters and black pudding, but look out also for some of the different German and Italian sausages and try using these occasionally. For those who like kidneys I have included a couple of recipes for these.

Marinated lamb chops

Cooking time 15-20 minutes + 2-3 hours marinating
Working time 15 minutes

For the marinade:

1 glass red wine	thyme
2 tablespoons oil	basil
1 dessertspoon wine vinegar	1 clove garlic, crushed
1 small onion, chopped	salt and pepper
1 teaspoon grated lemon rind	
½ teaspoon dry mustard	2-4 lamb chops (chump *or* loin)

Mix together all the ingredients for the marinade. The amount of basil and thyme is largely a matter of personal taste, but a sprinkling of each should be sufficient (it never does to be too heavy-handed with herbs). Put the lamb chops into a porcelain or pottery dish (marinating should never be done in a metal container), cover with the marinade and leave for 2-3 hours, turning occasionally. Remove the chops from the marinade and fry in a good non-stick pan. Very little, if any, extra fat should be required as the fat in the chops is usually sufficient. Seal the chops quickly on both sides, then lower the heat and fry for a further 8-12 minutes, depending on the size and thickness of the chops.

Serving suggestion: Serve with an interesting vegetable dish such as Menestra or Savoyarde potatoes (see pages 140 and 132) and carrots (see page 133).

Casseroled lamb

Cooking time 1¼ hours Working time 15 minutes

¼ kg (½ lb) lamb
1 tablespoon oil
2 cloves garlic, chopped
150 g (6 oz) shallots, chopped
150 g (6 oz) carrots, cut
  lengthwise

1 glass red wine *or* dry cider
bouquet garni
salt and pepper

Cut up the lamb and brown in the oil. Add the chopped garlic and shallots and the sliced carrots and sauté gently for about 5 minutes. Pour in the wine and put in the bouquet garni. Season with salt and pepper. Cover the casserole and cook over a low heat for 1 hour.

Lamb ossabucca

Cooking time 35 minutes Working time 20 minutes

2 stalks celery
1 carrot
knob of butter
flour
2-4 lamb chops
1 tablespoon oil

¼ litre (½ pint) stock
pinch each of oregano, thyme,
    rosemary and basil
1 tablespoon tomato purée
salt and pepper

Slice the celery finely, dice the carrot and sauté gently in the butter until softened. Remove and put aside on a plate. Put a few tablespoons of flour into a plastic bag and in this shake the lamb chops until they are evenly coated. Put the oil into the pan and fry the lamb chops for 2-3 minutes on each side. Add the stock, herbs, tomato purée and return the vegetables to the pan. Season with salt and pepper. Cover and cook gently for 20 minutes.

Serving suggestion: Serve with braised celery (see page 145) and puréed potatoes (see page 130).

Castilian lamb

Cooking time 40-50 minutes Working time 20-25 minutes

¼ kg (½ lb) lamb
1 medium onion
2-3 tomatoes
1 rasher streaky bacon
1 tablespoon lard, oil *or* butter
1 clove garlic
salt and pepper

a few almonds, grated (optional)
saffron
marjoram, thyme and bayleaf
1 dessertspoon flour
water
2-3 potatoes, peeled and thickly
    sliced
100 g (4 oz) peas

Cut the meat into squares. Chop the onion finely. Peel and chop the tomatoes. Dice the bacon and fry gently in the fat or oil. Turn up the heat a little and add the meat, onion and the whole clove of garlic. When they are browned, lower the heat again, remove the garlic and add the tomatoes and the salt and pepper. If using the grated almonds, add them to the pan with the saffron and the herbs. Sprinkle the contents of the pan with a little flour and just cover with water. Bring to the boil, lower the heat, cover and simmer for 15 minutes. Then add the peeled and sliced potatoes, and the peas if they are fresh, and cook for a further 20-25 minutes until the potatoes are cooked. If the peas are frozen, they must obviously be added in the last few minutes according to the instructions on the packet.

Juniper lamb stew

Cooking time 1¼ hours Working time 20 minutes

¼ kg (½ lb) boneless lamb (leg *or* shoulder)
1-2 tablespoons oil
1 onion, quartered
1 clove garlic, chopped
1 glass red wine (optional)

water
3 juniper berries
black peppercorns
bouquet garni
salt

Cut the lamb into cubes. Heat the oil in a casserole and brown the meat well. Add the quartered onion and the chopped garlic. Fry for a further minute or two, then add the wine and enough water to cover. In a pestle crush the juniper berries and a few black peppercorns. Put these into the casserole with the bouquet garni and salt to taste. Cover and cook over a moderate heat for 1 hour.

Serving suggestion: If you have two rings, new potatoes and baby carrots may be cooked separately. If your facilities are more limited just add these to the stew after 30 minutes. I personally prefer them this way.

Lamb sofrito

Sofrito is the past participle of the Spanish irregular verb *sofreir*. *Freir* means to fry and *sofreir* means to fry slightly. Thus *sofrito* is anything that is slightly fried. However, this dish or rather method of cooking is more traditionally associated with

Middle Eastern cookery. This is a very good way of cooking a leg of lamb if you do not have an oven. The recipe below serves 4 to 6 people depending on the size of the leg, but may be kept and served cold or used in a risotto if you want it just for the two of you.

Cooking time 2-3 hours Working time 15 minutes

3 tablespoons oil *or* butter	1 teaspoon oregano
1 leg of lamb	juice of ½ lemon
salt	water
freshly milled pepper	2 aubergines (optional)

Heat the oil in a large pan and put in the leg of lamb. Turn it until it is browned on all sides, then sprinkle with salt, freshly milled pepper, the oregano and lemon juice. Moisten with just a glass or two of water. Cover the pan and cook over a very low heat for 2-3 hours until the meat is very tender. If using a pan that does not have a very close-fitting lid, you will need to add a little extra water from time to time. Add the aubergines if desired for the last hour.

Serving suggestion: Serve with Provençale mushrooms (see page 144) and Mexican sweetcorn (see page 141).

Breton shoulder of lamb

Serves 4 Cooking time 1½ hours Working time 30 minutes

1 shoulder of lamb (boned)	*For garnish:*
pork fat	¼ kg (½ lb) haricot beans (soaked overnight)
1 onion, chopped	
3 cloves of garlic, chopped	1 onion, chopped
1-2 tomatoes, peeled and chopped	3-4 tomatoes, peeled and chopped
1 glass red wine	1 clove garlic, crushed
bouquet garni	olive oil
salt	2 tablespoons chopped parsley

Get your butcher to bone and roll the shoulder of lamb. Brown the lamb in pork fat with the chopped onion and garlic and the peeled and chopped tomatoes. Add the wine, bouquet garni and salt. Cover and cook slowly for 1 hour.

Meanwhile, cook the haricot beans (see page 102) until tender and prepare a mixture of the onion, tomatoes and garlic fried gently in olive oil. Mix in the parsley at the last minute and add the mixture to the drained beans. Serve the sauce from the cooking of the lamb in a separate sauceboat.

Lemon lamb

Cooking time 1 hour 20 minutes Working time 20-25 minutes

¼ kg (½ lb) boned leg of lamb
1 tablespoon olive oil
½ onion
1 clove garlic

1 level dessertspoon paprika
1 level dessertspoon chopped
  parsley
1 dessertspoon lemon juice
salt and pepper

Chop the meat into small cubes. Heat the oil and when it is beginning to smoke add the meat and sauté. When the pieces are browned remove them and put aside on a plate. Finely chop the onion and garlic and cook in the juice in the pan until they are transparent but not golden. Add the paprika, then the meat, parsley, lemon juice, salt and pepper. Cover tightly and simmer gently for 1 hour or until the meat is tender. Adjust the seasoning and serve.

Serving suggestion: Courgettes make a good accompaniment to this dish.

Pork chops in fino

Cooking time 30-35 minutes Working time 20 minutes

oil
1 onion, sliced
crushed black peppercorns
2 pork chops
a little hot paprika

a little sweet *or* cayenne paprika
mixed herbs
½ glass fino (very pale dry) sherry

Heat enough oil to just cover the base of a frying pan, add the sliced onion and cook until soft with a few crushed peppercorns. Remove. Season the pork chops on one side with the paprika and a few mixed herbs and seal first on the seasoned side. Season the other side and seal. Fry gently for a further 10-15 minutes, then return the onions to the pan and warm through thoroughly. Add the sherry and turn up the heat so that the sauce bubbles fast for a minute or two.

Serving suggestion: Serve with ratatouille (see page 138) or the mushroom and onion dish on page 144.

Pork chops in white wine and orange

Cooking time 30-35 minutes Working time 10-15 minutes

2 pork chops
oregano
oil

1 glass white wine
2 slices of orange

Sprinkle the pork chops with the oregano. Heat a little oil in a frying pan and seal and brown the chops on both sides. Fry gently for a further 10-15 minutes, then add the wine and the slices of orange. Turn up the heat and cook quickly for 5 minutes to reduce the sauce.

Serving suggestion: A good accompaniment to this dish would be boiled new potatoes tossed in butter and chopped parsley.

Pork fillets à la plancha

A la plancha in Spanish literally means 'on the plate' or 'by the plate method', which in this sense means a hot plate or griddle on which the meat is cooked directly. However, this recipe can be done equally well in a frying pan. The fillets should be thin for this method of cooking, as otherwise they will not cook through in this time.

Cooking time 10 minutes Working time 10 minutes

2 thinly sliced pork fillets	juice of ½ lemon
oil	2 slices of lemon

Paint the fillets with a little oil on both sides so that they will not stick. Heat the hot plate or frying pan and quickly seal the meat on both sides. Add the lemon juice, lower the heat a little and cook for 5 minutes. Garnish with the slices of lemon.

Serving suggestion: Serve with Triana-style French beans (see page 135).

Pork in cider

Cooking time 45 minutes Working time 30 minutes

1 onion	2 pieces of pork tenderloin *or* 2
½ green pepper	pork chops *or* fillets
½ red pepper	oregano
oil *or* fat	mild paprika
knob of butter	cayenne pepper
mushrooms	mixed herbs
	cider

Slice the onion and peppers. Heat the oil or fat in a smallish frying pan and add the sliced vegetables. When they are soft and the onions slightly golden, remove and put aside. Slice the mushrooms (3-4 largish ones is about right, but more or less can be used according to taste). Put a knob of butter in the pan and gently fry the mushrooms until they are soft but not shrivelled. Remove and put aside with the onion and peppers.

Season the pork with the oregano and spices, going very carefully with the cayenne. Add the pork to the pan and seal quickly on the seasoned side, sprinkling the upper side with a few mixed herbs. Turn and seal the other side. Fry for about 5 minutes. Pour over the cider so that it doesn't quite cover the pork. Bubble fiercely for 2 minutes. Add the vegetables and simmer gently for a further 10-15 minutes, depending on the thickness of the pork. They must not bleed when speared with a fork or knife.

Serving suggestion: Serve with French fried potatoes (see page 129).

Fruity pork

Cooking time 40-45 minutes Working time 15-20 minutes

knob of butter
2 pork chops
1 glass fresh orange juice
1 dessertspoon brown sugar
½ teaspoon mixed spice

a few drops soy sauce
1 apple
1 orange
a few black grapes *or* black
  cherries

Melt the butter in a frying pan. Add the chops and brown on both sides. While they are frying, mix the orange juice, brown sugar, mixed spice and soy sauce until they are well blended. Pour this mixture over the chops in the pan, then cover and simmer for 30 minutes. Meanwhile, slice the apple and orange and remove the pips or stones from the grapes or cherries. Turn the chops at fairly frequent intervals, so that the juice covers them. 10 minutes before serving, add the fruit.

Serving suggestion: Serve with savoury rice (see page 114) and a green salad.

Stuffed fillet of pork

Cooking time 45-55 minutes Working time 25 minutes

For the stuffing:
75 g (3 oz) kidney
30 g (good oz) soft white
  breadcrumbs
1 dessertspoon sherry
salt and pepper
2-4 thinly cut pork fillets

seasoned flour
1 small onion
100 g (4 oz) button mushrooms
knob of butter
¼ litre (½ pint) cider
2 tablespoons double cream

Chop the kidney as finely as possible (better still put it in a blender) and mix with the breadcrumbs and sherry. Season with salt and pepper. Spread this mixture on to the fillets, then roll up and secure with thread. Coat these in seasoned flour.

Slice the onion and mushrooms. Melt the butter and gently brown the fillets. Add the onion and mushrooms and cook for a further few minutes, then pour over the cider and the cream. Simmer for 45 minutes. Remove the thread round the fillets before serving with the sauce poured over.

Serving suggestion: Creamed potatoes are a good accompaniment to this dish.

Pork with lemon

Cooking time 30-35 minutes Working time 20 minutes

½ kg (1 lb) pork fillet
25 g (1 oz) lard
150 ml (¼ pint) dry white wine
2 level teaspoons ground cumin
1 clove garlic, crushed
salt

freshly crushed or milled black
  peppercorns
3 slices of lemon, cut into
  quarters
1 level teaspoon ground coriander

Trim away any fat there is on the pork and cut the meat into cubes. Melt the lard in a pan, add the meat and brown on all sides, turning occasionally. Stir in half the wine and add the cumin and crushed garlic. Season to taste with salt and pepper. Bring the mixture to the boil, cover and simmer over a low heat for 25 minutes or until the meat is tender. Add the rest of the wine and the lemon slices and cook for a further 5 minutes, then stir in the coriander. The sauce may be thickened with a little flour (mixed with cold water first).

Serving suggestion: Serve with boiled rice with a few cumin seeds added to the water during boiling, and a side salad of celery, walnut and orange (see page 158).

Pork sausages with barbecue sauce

Cooking time 30 minutes Working time 20 minutes

For the sauce:	
1 small onion	pinch chilli pepper
1-2 dessertspoons olive oil	dash of Worcester sauce
1 small tin tomatoes	salt
1 bayleaf	freshly milled pepper
1 clove garlic, crushed	$\frac{1}{4}$ kg ($\frac{1}{2}$ lb) pork sausages
rind of $\frac{1}{2}$ orange	25 g (1 oz) lard

Chop the onion and sauté in the oil until softened. Add the tinned tomatoes (which may be cut up in the pan – watching you don't ruin your Teflon!), the bayleaf, crushed garlic, orange rind, chilli powder and Worcester sauce. Season with salt and pepper. Cover and simmer gently for 30 minutes, then purée in a blender or pass through a sieve.

After the sauce has been cooking for about 15 minutes start to fry the sausages in the lard. Don't forget to prick them to stop them bursting and fry them gently at first to ensure they are cooked through. When they are done to your taste reheat the puréed sauce and pour over the sausages.

Serving suggestion: Serve with crusty bread and a salad.

Note: This sauce is also delicious with pork steak or gammon.

Frankfurter special

A slightly unusual dish, this is nevertheless incredibly simple to make and very quick as it requires virtually no cooking. The frankfurter and corn are really being warmed through and absorbing some of the flavour from the onions and cider.

Cooking time 20 minutes Working time 10 minutes

2 large onions	1 wine glass cider
1 tablespoon oil	salt and pepper
25 g (1 oz) butter	1 small tub soured cream
4-6 frankfurters	
1 small tin sweetcorn (with · peppers) drained	

Slice the onions and fry gently in the oil and butter in a frying pan. While these are cooking cut the frankfurters into pieces about 2-3 cm (1-1½ in) long. When the onion is softened, add the frankfurter pieces to the pan, and fry for a further 5 minutes. Add the drained sweetcorn and the cider and simmer for 10 minutes. Season with salt and pepper and stir in the soured cream just before serving.

Serving suggestion: Serve with new potatoes, green lentils or pasta shells.

Sausage and onion casserole

Cooking time 45-50 minutes Working time 15-20 minutes

¼ kg (½ lb) sausages	1 dessertspoon flour
knob of lard	¼ litre (½ pint) brown ale *or*
1 onion	Guinness
50-100 g (2-4 oz) mushrooms	¼ litre (½ pint) stock
knob of butter	salt and pepper
½ teaspoon dry mustard	

Fry the sausages in the lard. Remove from the pan and chop each sausage into three or four pieces. Slice the onion and mushrooms and in the same pan, adding a little extra butter if necessary, fry these gently until softened. Stir in the mustard powder and the flour and cook for 1 minute. Add the brown ale and the stock and then return the sausages to the pan. Season with salt and pepper and cook, covered, for 30 minutes.

Serving suggestion: Serve with new potatoes or noodles.

Black pudding with apple sauce

Cooking time 15-20 minutes Working time 10 minutes

For the sauce:	sugar to taste (approx. 1-2
2 apples	dessert spoons)
a little water	25 g (1 oz) butter
	½ kg (1 lb) black pudding

Peel, core and slice the apples. Put into a saucepan with a very little water. Cover and cook gently until the apples are softened, but not mushy. Add the sugar and cook for a further minute or two. Put aside.

Melt the butter in a pan and add the black pudding and fry gently for 5 minutes. As black pudding is a type of sausage which has already been cooked it does not really require much more than heating through thoroughly. Reheat the sauce and pour over.

Serving suggestion: Serve with plain boiled or puréed potatoes (see page 130).

Pigs' kidneys with mushrooms, peppers and white wine

Cooking time 30 minutes Working time 10-15 minutes + 1 hour soaking

2 pigs' kidneys
25 g (1 oz) butter
2 small rashers bacon, diced
3-4 mushrooms, sliced
1 sweet red pepper, sliced

1 glass white wine
4 tablespoons meat stock
chopped parsley
bouquet garni
salt and pepper

Soak the kidneys in warm salted water for 1 hour. Cut them transversally into slices about 1 cm ($\frac{1}{2}$ in) thick. Melt the butter in a saucepan. Add the diced bacon and the kidneys and cook gently for 1 minute. Add the sliced mushrooms and red pepper. Fry for a few minutes and then turn up the heat, add the wine and allow it to bubble for a minute or two. Lower the heat, add the remaining ingredients and simmer gently, covered, for 15 minutes.

Serving suggestion: Serve sprinkled with parsley on a bed of rice or with Mousseline potatoes (see page 130).

Kidneys with sherry

Cooking time 20-25 minutes Working time 10 minutes

2 calves' or pigs' kidneys
butter
3-4 mushrooms, sliced
1 glass fino sherry
1-2 large potatoes peeled and sliced

4-5 tablespoons stock
1 clove garlic, crushed or chopped
salt and pepper

Prepare the kidneys as in the previous recipe. Melt a little butter in a pan and sauté the kidneys and sliced mushrooms for a few minutes. Pour over the sherry and bring to the boil. Boil rapidly until the liquid is reduced to half. Add the stock, the crushed garlic and the peeled and sliced potato. Season, with salt and pepper. Cover and simmer gently for a further 10-15 minutes.

Serving suggestion: Serve with a side salad and some French bread to mop up the juice.

Lambs' hearts

Cooking time 30-35 minutes Working time 15-20 minutes

2 large carrots	juice of ½ lemon
1 large *or* 2 medium onions	pinch of ground coriander
2 lambs' hearts	pinch of cumin seeds
1 tablespoon olive oil	pinch of rosemary
knob of butter	salt and pepper
6-7 tablespoons water	

Slice the carrots and chop the onions. Cut the hearts into cubes or slices. Heat the oil and butter in a pan and sauté the vegetables and the hearts for 5 minutes. Cover the pan and continue cooking for a further 5 minutes over a gentle heat. Add the water, lemon juice, coriander, cumin and rosemary. Season, then re-cover and cook gently for a further 20 minutes. Do make sure if your pan lid is not close-fitting that the water does not all evaporate! Add a little extra water if necessary. This dish does not have a lot of sauce. If you prefer something less dry, it is better to use ¼ litre (½ pint) of stock to add a little flavour rather than just using water.

Serving suggestion: Serve this with plain boiled or saffron rice (see page 108).

5 Chicken

Chicken has the advantage these days of being reasonably cheap and also quite quick to cook. Frozen chickens are not, however, always full of flavour and so often seem to need a little bit of 'tarting up' to make the best of them. In the following chapter I put forward various suggestions for doing just that, varying from curry, often unjustly regarded as the ultimate disguise, through casseroles with wine to a delicious marinated then deep-fried chicken dish. If you are using frozen chicken, do allow several hours for it to defrost, otherwise you will find that the meat near the bone is undercooked and chicken is not a meat that people expect served a delicate pink!

Fruity chicken curry

Cooking time 1 hour 20 minutes (on the bone)
1 hour 40 minutes (off the bone) Working time 20-25 minutes.

2 chicken legs	½ tablespoon flour
1-2 tablespoons olive oil	2 tomatoes, peeled and chopped
½ litre (1 pint) water	handful of raisins
1 bayleaf	2-3 cardamoms, crushed
salt and pepper	a few cumin seeds
1 small onion	2 rings pineapple
1 clove garlic	1 banana
1 small apple	juice of ½ lemon
1 heaped tablespoon curry	
powder	

The chicken for this dish can be treated in one of two ways; it can be either used on or off the bone. I personally prefer it off the bone and give that method below. However, if your preference is for meat on the bone then the legs should be first fried in the oil, then removed whilst the onion and apple are fried and the curry added, and then returned to the pan to cook in the sauce when the stock is added.

For the other method, pre-cook the chicken by frying in a little oil. Pour off any excess oil and add the water, bayleaf, salt and pepper and cook for 30-40 minutes. Remove and take the meat off the bone, reserving the stock for the curry.

Chop the onion and garlic. Peel, core and slice the apple. Fry the onions in oil until soft. Add the apple and fry for a further 2 minutes, then add the curry powder and flour. Cook for another 2 minutes then add the chicken stock, garlic, peeled and chopped tomatoes, raisins, crushed cardamoms and cumin seeds. Cover and cook for 30 minutes, then add the chopped pineapple and the chicken. Cook for a futher 15 minutes, then add the sliced banana and lemon juice. After another 10 minutes the dish is ready.

Serving suggestion: Serve with plain boiled or saffron rice (see page 108) and have a dish of mango chutney and a dish of desiccated coconut on the table.

Chicken fricassee

Cooking time 1 hour Working time 20 minutes

2 chicken breasts *or* legs
oil
150 ml (¼ pint) water
1 bayleaf
1 small onion
150 g (6 oz) mushrooms
1 clove garlic

50 g (2 oz) butter
2 level tablespoons flour
150 ml (¼ pint) milk
salt
freshly milled pepper
juice of ½ lemon

Pre-cook the chicken as in the previous recipe but using only 150 ml (¼ pint) water. Reserve the stock.

Slice the onion and chop the mushrooms and garlic. Melt half the butter in a pan and fry the onion, mushrooms and garlic until they are soft. Add the remaining butter, the flour, milk and reserved stock. Season with salt and pepper. Bring to the boil, whisking continuously, and boil for 2-3 minutes. Add the chicken which has been taken off the bone and the lemon juice.

Serving suggestion: Serve with peas and sweetcorn mixed and plain boiled rice.

Chicken Andaluz

Cooking time 1 hour Working time 15-20 minutes

1 onion
1 red *or* green pepper

4-5 large tomatoes
1 clove garlic

1½ tablespoons olive oil
2 chickens legs *or* breasts
12 olives

1 glass fino sherry
chopped parsley

Slice the onion and the pepper. Peel and chop the tomatoes and chop the garlic. Sauté all these ingredients with the chicken in the oil, which should be hot. If the olives are bitter, they should be blanched first; if not, simply stone and then add to the ingredients in the pan. Cover and cook gently for 40 minutes. Pour the sherry over the chicken and cook for a further 10 minutes

To garnish, sprinkle with chopped parsley.

Serving suggestion: Serve with plain boiled or saffron rice (see page 108).

Chicken Manolo

Cooking time 40-45 minutes Working time 15 minutes

1 small onion
150 g (6 oz) mushrooms
50 g (2 oz) butter
2 chicken breasts
salt and pepper

1 glass amontillado sherry
2 tablespoons double cream
paprika
1 tablespoon chopped parsley

Chop the onion and slice the mushrooms. Heat the butter in a pan and gently cook these ingredients until tender. Remove and put aside. Skin the chicken breasts and shallow fry in the same pan until the meat is cooked. When they are ready the meat will start to draw away from the bone, but test with a skewer to make sure that the meat is cooked all the way through. Return the onions and mushrooms to the pan, season with salt and pepper, then pour in the sherry and flame. Add the cream, sprinkle with paprika and serve as soon as the cream is heated through and beginning to thicken. Garnish with the chopped parsley.

Serving suggestion: Serve with fried peppers (see page 137).

Chicken cider casserole

Cooking time 1 hour 20 minutes Working time 25 minutes

25 g (1 oz) butter	2 carrots
2 chicken portions	1 level dessertspoon flour
2 onions	¼ litre (scant ½ pint) dry cider
1 stick celery	bouquet garni
150 g (6 oz) mushrooms	salt and pepper

Heat the butter in a pan and fry the chicken until well browned. Quarter the onions, chop the celery and add to the pan with the whole mushrooms. Fry gently for a few minutes, adding a little extra butter if necessary. Slice the carrots and add these to the other ingredients. Stir in the flour and add the cider and bouquet garni. Season with salt and pepper. Bring to the boil, lower the heat, cover and simmer gently for 45 minutes or until the meat is tender.

Serving suggestion: Serve with braised chicory (see page 146) and a side salad.

Somerset chicken

Cider and apples are most usually associated with pork, but are used in this recipe to form a delicious accompaniment to chicken.

Cooking time 1 hour Working time 20-25 minutes

1 eating apple	2 chicken joints
50 g (2 oz) butter	200 ml (⅓ pint) dry cider
1 tablespoon flour	1-2 tablespoons double cream
salt and pepper	wedges of lemon

Peel and core the apple and cut into slices. Melt the butter in a frying pan and fry the apple slices gently for 3-4 minutes. Remove and put aside on a plate. Season the flour with a little salt and pepper. Remove the skin from the chicken and coat in the seasoned flour. (I always do this operation in a plastic bag.) Put the chicken joints in the pan and fry until the outside is a pale golden brown. Add the cider, cover and simmer for 40-45 minutes or until the chicken is tender. Stir in the cream and return the apple to the pan. Heat through gently before serving garnished with lemon wedges.

Chicken with orange

Cooking time 1 hour Working time 30 minutes

1 level tablespoon butter	2 oranges
1 tablespoon olive oil	salt and pepper
2 chicken legs	1 heaped teaspoon flour
1 tablespoon concentrated stock	hot water

Heat the butter and oil in a pan and fry the chicken pieces until golden. Add the stock, the grated rind of 1 orange, salt and pepper and the flour mixed with a little cold water. Cover and cook for 40 minutes, gradually adding hot water, and the juice of 1 orange until a thick sauce is produced. Cut the rind of the other orange into fine julienne strips, being careful not to include the pith. Put the strips into boiling water for 3 minutes and add them to the casserole 5 minutes before the end. Finally, add the segments of the second orange and turn them well in the sauce.

Serving suggestion: Freshly cooked leaf spinach (see page 134) makes a good accompanying vegetable.

Coq au vin

Cooking time 1 hour Working time 20 minutes

50 g (2 oz) butter
1 tablespoon olive oil
2 chicken legs
2 rashers streaky bacon
12 shallots
12 button mushrooms

¼ bottle burgundy
1 clove garlic, crushed
bouquet garni
chopped parsley
salt and pepper

Melt the butter in a pan with the oil and brown the chicken legs. Remove and put aside. Remove the rinds and dice the bacon. Slice the shallots. Add the shallots and the bacon to the pan and cook for a few minutes, then add the whole mushrooms. Fry gently for 5-10 minutes. Return the chicken to the pan. Pour in the wine, add the crushed garlic, the bouquet garni and seasoning. Bring to the boil, lower the heat, cover and cook gently for about 40 minutes. The sauce may need thickening at the end with a little kneaded butter. Serve sprinkled with chopped parsley.

Serving suggestion: Sauté potatoes (see page 130) go well with this dish.

Chicken paprika

A proper Hungarian version of this dish. It depends, as do so many Hungarian recipes, on having available soured cream, which is used to thicken and flavour the sauce.

Cooking time 1 hour 15 minutes Working time 15-20 minutes

potatoes
2 chicken legs *or* breasts
salt
knob of lard

1 red onion, chopped
Hungarian paprika (hot)
a few drops of wine vinegar
stock
soured cream

Wash the amount of potatoes required and boil in their skins in salted water. Test with a fork to see when they are done, then peel and put aside. Wash the chicken pieces and sprinkle with salt. Melt the lard in a pan, add the chopped onion and fry until soft. Stir in a little paprika and a few drops of vinegar. Add the chicken pieces and fry lightly without browning. Add a little stock, cover and stew for 40-45 minutes, shaking the pan occasionally to make sure that the chicken and onions are not sticking. Finally, add a good dessertspoon of soured cream and the prepared potatoes. The mixture may, if desired, be coloured by the method described in the recipe for Hungarian goulash (see page 48).

Serving suggestion: Any plain vegetable such as French beans goes well with this recipe.

Hungarian chicken casserole

Another very similar Hungarian dish – the main difference being the addition of tomato purée and mushrooms. The paprika used here is the sweet kind.

Cooking time 1 hour Working time 15 minutes

½ red onion	stock
knob of lard	new potatoes
2 chicken legs *or* breasts	1 tablespoon soured cream
Hungarian paprika (sweet)	chopped parsley
100 g (4 oz) mushrooms	salt
1 large tablespoon tomato purée	

Chop the onion and fry in the lard. Add the chicken and a good heaped teaspoon of paprika once the onions are beginning to soften. Slice the mushrooms. When the chicken is browned add the tomato purée, mushrooms and enough stock or water to cover. Clean the new potatoes and add these to the casserole with a pinch of salt. Cook for 45 minutes-1 hour and just before serving, stir in the soured cream. Sprinkle with chopped parsley.

Nutty sweet and sour chicken

Cooking time 1 hour 10 minutes Working time 30 minutes

25 g (1 oz) breadcrumbs
25 g (1 oz) peanuts, chopped
25 g (1 oz) almonds, chopped
50 g (2 oz) chestnut purée
2 chicken breasts
4 rashers streaky bacon
25 g (1 oz) butter

For the sauce:
1 small onion

½ green pepper
knob of butter
1 small carrot, grated
2-3 pineapple rings, cubed
1 tablespoon tomato purée
pinch of mixed herbs
salt and pepper
1 dessertspoon cornflour
¼ litre (½ pint) apple juice

Mix together the breadcrumbs, peanuts, almonds and chestnut purée. Slit the chicken joints by making an opening lengthwise and stuff with the purée mixture. Wrap two bacon rashers round each joint and tie on. Heat the butter gently in a frying pan and brown the chicken breasts.

In another pan make the sauce. Slice the onion and green pepper and fry in the butter. Add the grated carrot, pineapple cubes, tomato purée and herbs. Season with salt and pepper. Cook for 5 minutes over a low heat, then mix in the cornflour and slowly pour in the apple juice. Drain any excess fat there may be in the pan with the chicken and pour the sauce over. Cover and simmer gently for 40 minutes.

Serving suggestion: Serve with rice.

Cucumber chicken

Cooking time 45-50 minutes Working time 20 minutes

1 small onion
1 medium potato
4 chicken drumsticks
knob of butter
4 glasses water
2 glasses white wine

1 chicken stock cube
1 bayleaf
salt and pepper
2 tablespoons cream
100 g (4 oz) cucumber, peeled
    and cubed

Finely chop the onion and peel and dice the potato. Brown the chicken in the butter for 5 minutes, then add the onion. When the chicken is well browned add the water, wine, stock cube bayleaf and the potato. Season with salt and pepper. Cover and simmer for 30 minutes, then remove the chicken. Whisk the pan liquor until smooth, then add the cream and peeled and cubed cucumber. Adjust the seasoning and pour over the chicken.

Serving suggestion: Serve with new potatoes.

Stuffed chicken

This is not a dish that can be made for two, but it is delicious and my excuse for including it is that if there are only two of you, the remainder is excellent served cold with a salad the following day.

Serves 4-6 Cooking time 1 hour 40 minutes Working time 35 minutes

1 roasting chicken	½ teaspoon salt
100 g (4 oz) ham, chopped	freshly milled pepper
¼ kg (½ lb) pork, minced	3 tablespoons lemon juice
50 g (2 oz) bacon, diced	1 egg, beaten
50 g (2 oz) fine breadcrumbs	3-4 tablespoons oil
1 tablespoon chopped parsley	¼ litre (scant ½ pint) white wine
2 cloves garlic, minced	or sherry (optional)
¼ teaspoon grated nutmeg	3-4 tablespoons water *or* stock
½ teaspoon oregano	

Clean the chicken for stuffing. In a bowl mix the chopped ham, minced pork and diced bacon. Add the breadcrumbs, chopped parsley, minced garlic, nutmeg, oregano, salt and pepper and lemon juice. Blend in the beaten egg. Stuff the chicken with this mixture. Sew up or skewer the opening and use string to keep the legs and wings in place. In a pot heat the oil and slowly brown the chicken over a medium heat.

When golden, add any remaining stuffing to the pot with the wine and water. Cover and simmer for 1½ hours or until the chicken is very tender.

Serving suggestion: Serve with saffron rice (see page 108) and bean shoots and orange salad (see page 153).

Chicken in mushroom and brandy sauce

Cooking time 50 minutes Working time 20 minutes

1 large green pepper	water
150 g (6 oz) mushrooms	measure of brandy
2 cloves garlic	juice of 2 oranges
oil and butter	1 teaspoon honey
2 chicken legs *or* breasts	salt
½ packet mushroom soup	nutmeg
milk	cinnamon

Slice the green pepper and the mushrooms and chop the garlic. In a saucepan or frying pan with a lid, melt a little butter with some cooking oil. Brown the chicken for 5 minutes, then add the garlic, green pepper and mushrooms. Meanwhile, make up the ½ packet of mushroom soup, making it with half milk and half water and of a thicker consistency than usual.

When the chicken legs are well browned, pour off the excess fat in the pan. Warm the brandy (this is best done in a ladle which can be heated over a flame), ignite and pour slowly over the contents of the pan. When the flames have died down, add the orange juice, bubble for a minute, then add the soup mixture and the honey. Season with salt, nutmeg and cinnamon. Cook for a further 30 minutes.

Serving suggestion: Serve with rice and a green or mixed salad.

Chicken with cheese and mushroom sauce

Cooking time 50 minutes Working time 20 minutes

100-150 g (4-6 oz) mushrooms
2 cloves garlic
oil and butter
2 chicken legs *or* breasts
½ packet mushroom *or* other
  cream soup

½ carton soured cream
grated cheese to taste
nutmeg
salt
freshly milled pepper

This recipe is similar to the previous one.

Wash and cut up the mushrooms, and chop the garlic. In a saucepan or frying pan with a lid, melt a little butter with some cooking oil. Brown the chicken for 5 minutes, then add the mushrooms and garlic. Meanwhile, make up the ½ packet of soup using all water and with a thicker consistency than usual.

When the chicken pieces are well browned, pour off the excess fat. Add the soup mixture and stir in the soured cream. Add the grated cheese, and season with nutmeg, salt and pepper. Cover and cook for a further 30 minutes.

Serving suggestion: Serve with rice and a green salad.

Chicken parmesan drumsticks

Cooking time 40-45 minutes Working time 25 minutes

1 heaped tablespoon
  breadcrumbs
1 heaped tablespoon Parmesan
  cheese
salt and pepper
dash of Tabasco sauce

1 egg, beaten
4 chicken drumsticks
1 tablespoon oil
50 g (2 oz) butter

Mix together the breadcrumbs and cheese. Season with salt and pepper. Add a dash of Tabasco sauce to the beaten egg. Remove the skins from the drumsticks, dip in the beaten egg and then in the breadcrumb mixture. Heat the oil and butter in a frying pan and when the fat is hot but not smoking (the butter should not brown) put in the drumsticks and fry until golden on all sides. Lower the heat and cook for a further 20 minutes

Serving suggestion: Serve with French fries (see page 129) and a green salad.

Garlic chicken

Cooking time 10-15 minutes + 2-3 hours marinating
Working time 20-25 minutes

measure of brandy	flour
juice of 1 lemon	oil for deep-frying
1 teaspoon red pepper	watercress
2-4 cloves garlic, chopped	grated carrot
2 chicken breasts	slices of lemon
salt	

Mix together the brandy, lemon juice, red pepper and chopped garlic. Marinate the chicken in this mixture for 2-3 hours. Remove, drain well, season with salt and roll in flour. Fry in plenty of *hot* oil until golden. Test with a skewer to make sure the inside is done. Drain on kitchen paper. Garnish with watercress and grated carrot and slices of lemon.

Serving suggestion: French fries go very well with this dish and provided you have pre-cooked them (see page 130), they are a convenient thing to do as you already have the hot oil.

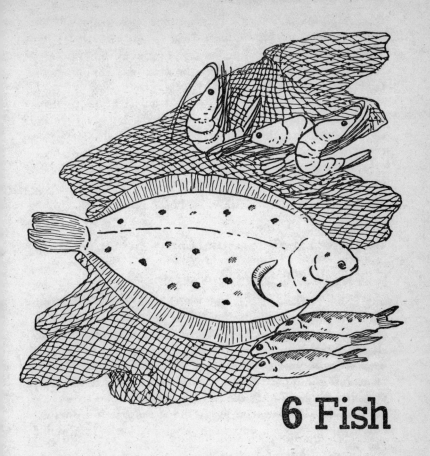

6 Fish

Obviously a whole book can, and has been, devoted to fish. The same applies to every section of this little handbook. I am giving here a fairly small selection of simple but varied recipes. Some of the types of fish are, it is true, not easily available in this country except in London – but in many cases the method of cooking can be adapted equally well to a different kind of fish.

When buying fresh fish, note that the eyes should be bright and not sunken and that the gills should be red, as these are indications of freshness.

Cleaning fish

Hold the fish by the tail and wash under cold running water, removing the scales by scraping the back of a knife from the tail towards the head.

If the fish has not been gutted, slit it just below the head along the belly to the vent and remove the intestines. In the case of small fish they can be cut across the shoulders thus removing head and intestines in one operation.

Cleaning squid is a rather different matter and the method is given later in this chapter, on page 000.

96

Deep-fried sardines, sprats or whitebait

Cooking time 10-15 minutes Working time 10-15 minutes

¼ kg (½ lb) of these fish is ample and provides a very good, tasty and cheap meal. The heads can be cut off before frying, but this is not strictly necessary if the fish are small. They should simply be rolled in seasoned flour and fried in plenty of deep fat until golden. The secret of deep-frying is always to make sure the fat is really hot. The best way to test it is by dropping in one fish. If the fish immediately floats to the top and bubbles furiously then the fat is hot enough. If it does not do this, then the fat is only ready when it starts to buzz round and bubble.

When the fish are ready, remove from the pan and drain off any excess fat before serving with plenty of fresh lemon to squeeze over. A salad is always a good accompaniment to this meal.

Note: Any fish may be deep-fried in this way. The flour, however, will not stick if the fat is not hot enough.

If you have not got sufficient fat to deep-fry, the fish may be shallow-fried, but this doesn't seem to produce the same, even, golden appearance. My preference for deep-frying is always a vegetable oil, usually sunflower, as this does not have any strong flavour of its own, as for example, soya or corn oil have.

Poached fish

This is a suitable way of cooking almost any fish, either white fish or the oily fish like herring or mackerel.

Cooking time 45 minutes-1 hour + 30 minutes for stock
Working time 25 minutes

½ kg (1 lb) fresh fish
¼ litre (scant ½ pint) fish stock *or*
   125 ml (¼ pint) stock and
   125 ml (¼ pint) white wine
a little extra oil *or* butter
30 g (1 oz) butter
1 tablespoon flour
2 tablespoons thick cream
1 egg yolk, beaten
wedges of lemon

chopped parsley

For the stock:
head, bones and skin of fish
¼ litre (½ pint) water
1 small onion, sliced
1 carrot, sliced
1-2 bayleaves
pinch of thyme
pinch of nutmeg

First prepare and clean the fish, then make the stock. Add all the fish trimmings to the water and other ingredients and simmer for 30 minutes, then strain. Rub the fish with oil or butter and lay in a pan. Pour over the stock, or stock and wine. Simmer gently until the fish is tender, basting if necessary. Meanwhile, make a roux by melting the butter in a saucepan and blending in the flour with a wooden spoon. Take this off the heat after a few minutes and when the fish is cooked return to the heat, warm gently and add to this the liquid the fish has cooked in. Beat the cream gently into the egg yolk, and add this mixture to the sauce. Pour the sauce over the fish and serve garnished with lemon wedges and chopped parsley.

Serving suggestion: Serve with new potatoes.

Catalan fish

This recipe was passed on by a Catalonian woman who lived in our block of flats. She told me it was a traditional way of cooking small fish. Like all the recipes I was given in Spain, no mention was made of quantities so the ratios below are fairly arbitrary. It is a dish which could equally well be used for fillets or steaks of larger fish.

Cooking time 20-30 minutes Working time 20-30 minutes

3-4 tomatoes	oil
1 clove garlic	salt and pepper
1 green *or* red pepper	4-6 small fish
2 small aubergines	juice of ½ lemon
chopped parsley	

Peel and chop the tomatoes. Mince the garlic and chop the pepper. Slice the aubergines, sprinkle with salt and leave with a plate on to drain for 15 minutes. When ready, add a good amount of roughly chopped parsley and gently fry all these ingredients together in plenty of oil, preferably olive oil. Season with salt and pepper. Shallow-fry the little fish and arrange on a dish. Cover with the vegetable mixture and squeeze the lemon juice over the top.

Mackerel in cider

This is a dish which is more usually done in the oven, but can be done equally well on the top of the cooker. The recipe is suitable for herring, trout and whiting as well as mackerel.

Cooking time 45 minutes Working time 10 minutes

2 dessert apples	1 bayleaf
1 small onion	salt
2 mackerel	freshly milled pepper
150 ml (¼ pint) cider	juice of ½ lemon

Peel, core and slice the apples. Slice the onion. Clean the fish, but leave the heads on. Put into a pan, cover with the onion and apple, pour over the cider, add the bayleaf and season with the salt and freshly milled pepper. Add the lemon juice. Cover the pan with a close-fitting lid, or if the pan does not have one, cover closely with aluminium foil. Cook gently for 45 minutes or until the fish are tender. This dish may be served hot or cold.

Serving suggestion: Serve with brown bread and butter and a mixed salad (see page 152).

Nutty fish

Cooking time 20-30 minutes + 20 minutes marinating
Working time 20-30 minutes

300 g (12 oz) white fish fillets
1 tablespoon lemon juice
1 teaspoon grated lemon rind
flour
salt
freshly milled pepper

50 g (2 oz) butter and oil
40 g (1½ oz) peanuts or cashew
  nuts, chopped
lemon wedges
chopped parsley

Marinate the fish fillets in the lemon juice and rind for 15-20 minutes. Season the flour with salt and freshly milled pepper and coat the fish with this. (I always do this in a plastic bag.) Heat the butter in a pan, adding just a little oil to help stop the butter from browning or burning. Fry the fish until tender. Remove and in the same pan, adding a little extra butter if necessary, fry the chopped nuts until lightly browned. Add the marinade and pour this mixture over the fish. Serve with lemon wedges and a sprinkling of chopped parsley.

Serving suggestion: Serve with fresh spinach (see page 134) or a bean shoots and orange salad (see page 153).

Fish fillets with vegetables

Cooking time 30 minutes Working time 15 minutes

½ Dutch cabbage
1 small onion
2 stalks celery
2-3 carrots
2-3 tomatoes
knob of butter
¼ kg (½ lb) white fish such as cod
  or haddock

1 tablespoon water
1 bayleaf
pinch each of oregano and thyme
salt
freshly milled pepper
1 teaspoon paprika pepper

Cut the cabbage into thin strips, chop the onion and celery and slice the carrots thinly. Peel and chop the tomatoes. Sauté all the vegetables gently in the butter until soft, about 10-15 minutes. Cut the fish into pieces, add to the pan with the vegetables and cook for a few minutes. Add the water, herbs and seasoning, cover the pan and simmer for 10-15 minutes until the fish is cooked.

Serving suggestion: Serve with Savoyarde potatoes (see page 132).

Steamed fish with parsley sauce

This dish is very simple to make and again, although one most people normally put into the oven, it is equally suited to doing on the top. If you really are juggling for space, it can even be done in a shallow tin plate on top of another saucepan, in which, for example, you are cooking the potatoes.

Cooking time 30 minutes Working time 15-20 minutes

¼ kg (½ lb) white fish
25 g (1 oz) butter
150 ml (¼ pint) milk
salt
freshly milled pepper

For the sauce:
20 g (¾ oz) butter
20 g (¾ oz) flour
¼ litre (scant ½ pint) milk
2 tablespoons chopped parsley

Lay the fish fillets in a pan, which may either be put directly over gentle heat, or preferably into another pan half filled with water *(bain-marie)*. Dot with butter, pour over the milk and season with a little salt and some freshly milled pepper.

While this is cooking, prepare the sauce. Melt the butter, remove from the heat and blend in the flour. Return the pan to the heat, cook gently for a few moments, then slowly add the milk. This way the sauce will not taste floury. Adding the milk requires patience and constant stirring, otherwise the sauce will end up lumpy. Once all the milk has been added, cook the sauce for a few minutes, adding a little extra milk or water if its consistency is too thick. Add the chopped parsley. Serve the fish with the sauce poured over it. The milk and butter mixture in which the fish has been cooked may be added to the parsley sauce or spooned over separately.

Serving suggestion: Serve with mashed potatoes.

Cod in tomato sauce

Salt cod has an unprepossessing appearance, but when it has been soaked it can form the basis of some very interesting dishes.

Cooking time 35 minutes + overnight soaking of salt cod
Working time 20 minutes

¼ kg (½ lb) salt *or* fresh cod

For the sauce:
½ kg (1 lb) tomatoes
1 small onion

1-2 tablespoons olive oil
1-2 cloves garlic
salt and pepper
1 bayleaf

If you are using salt cod, soak it overnight, change the water the following morning and leave to soak for a further few hours. Rinse well, remove the skin and bones and poach in water for 20 minutes. If using fresh cod, poach for 15 minutes. Flake and put aside.

To prepare the tomato sauce, immerse the tomatoes in boiling water for 1 minute to enable you to remove the skins easily, then peel and chop. Chop the onion finely and fry gently in the olive oil until well softened and just beginning to go golden. Add the crushed garlic, the tomatoes, salt and pepper and the bayleaf. Fry for 5 minutes, then cover and continue cooking over a low heat for 15-20 minutes until the tomatoes have been reduced to a purée. Either sieve or put the mixture into a blender. Return to the heat, adjust the seasoning, add the cod and cook for a further 10 minutes.

Serving suggestion: Serve with rice.

Honeyed fish

Cooking time 20-25 minutes Working time 15-20 minutes

350 g (12 oz) cod fillet
flour
salt and pepper
1-2 tablespoons olive oil
  or 25 g (1 oz) butter
pinch of rosemary

1 tablespoon clear honey
1 tablespoon pine or other nuts
1 tablespoon raisins
½ clove garlic, finely chopped
several tablespoons water
juice of 1 lemon

Wash and skin the cod fillet. Cut it into largish pieces and roll lightly in the flour, seasoned with salt and pepper. Melt the oil or butter in a pan, add a pinch of rosemary and sauté for 10-15 minutes until the fish is tender. Remove from the pan and drain any excess fat from the pan. Put in all the other ingredients, bring the mixture to the boil, return the fish to the pan, and simmer for 5 minutes before serving.

Serving suggestion: A green salad and some crusty bread are the ideal accompaniments to this dish.

Pickled herring

Cooking time 10 minutes Working time 20-25 minutes

2 herrings	1 teaspoon pickling spices
1 onion, finely sliced	*or* mixed whole spice
125 ml (¼ pint) vinegar	2-3 bayleaves
125 ml (¼ pint) water	12 peppercorns
1 dessertspoon brown sugar	3-4 thin slices of lemon
	soured cream or yoghurt

Clean the herrings thoroughly, removing the entrails, but do not remove the skin. They may then be sectioned or left whole. Place them with the finely sliced onion in a porcelain dish. In a saucepan bring to the boil the vinegar, water and sugar. Remove from the heat, add the spices, bayleaves, peppercorns and lemon slices, allow to cool slightly and pour over the herrings. Cover and allow to stand for 24 hours before serving. Serve with soured cream or yoghurt.

Serving suggestion: A cucumber salad (see page 155) goes well with these herrings.

Gambas al ajillo
Prawns garlic style

As you can see from the ingredients, you need to like garlic as well as prawns to like this dish!

To prepare and serve this, a small shallow earthenware dish is traditionally used, but a small saucepan or frying pan will do as well.

Cooking time 5-8 minutes Working time 15-20 minutes

¼ kg (½ lb) prawns	olive oil
3-4 cloves garlic	chopped parsley

Peel the prawns and remove the heads. (There is no quick, simple method of doing this! Like most seafood it requires time and patience – unless you choose the easy way out and buy pre-cooked frozen ones.) Chop the garlic finely. Heat a little olive oil in a pan and add the garlic and the prawns. Cook for 3-5 minutes. The prawns will have shrunk and the liquid they contained will have mixed with the oil and the garlic to form a sauce. Sprinkle with chopped parsley and serve immediately.

Serving suggestion: This is not really a main dish, but is usually served as a starter or as a *tapa,* an appetiser. Serve with fresh bread to mop up the juices.

Señor vizconde

Cooking time 10 minutes Working time 20-25 minutes

¼ kg (½ lb) fresh prawns	knob of butter
100 g (4 oz) ham	olive oil
150 g (6 oz) mushrooms	salt and pepper
3 cloves garlic	chopped parsley

Peel the prawns and remove the heads. Cut the ham into small squares or cubes. Slice the mushrooms and garlic and sauté in the butter. Add a little olive oil to the pan. When this is hot, add the prawns and the ham. Fry for 5 minutes. Season with a little salt and pepper, sprinkle with chopped parsley and serve immediately.

Note: A small amount of brandy which has been heated may be flamed and poured over the dish, but this is optional.

Mejillonada

Cooking time 25-30 minutes Working time 30 minutes

½ kg (1 lb) mussels *(mejillones)*	thyme
white wine	1 bayleaf
1 onion, chopped	1 clove garlic, chopped
1 clove *or* a little powdered clove	oil *or* butter
black peppercorns	1 tablespoon tomato purée
parsley	1 teaspoon cornflour

Wash the mussels. This must be done very thoroughly and any that are cracked or remain open after being tapped sharply should be discarded. Those that remain should be scrubbed and washed under running water and then rinsed in cold water to get rid of all sand and weed. Ideally, mussels should be cooked on the day they are purchased; if this is not possible then they should be covered with fresh cold water until they are used.

When the mussels are clean, bring them to the boil in a mixture of wine, half the chopped onion, clove, black peppercorns and herbs. When they open take them out and remove one half of each shell. Strain the cooking liquid and reserve. In a saucepan, soften the remaining onion and the chopped garlic in the oil or butter. Add the tomato purée and cornflour and pour in the reserved liquid from the mussels. Cook over a high heat for 3 minutes and serve in a casserole.

Mejillones à la marinera

Cooking time 15-20 minutes   Working time 30 minutes

½ kg (1 lb) mussels *or* clams	bouquet garni
1 glass white wine	1 shallot, finely chopped
1 glass water	chopped parsley

It is essential that mussels are alive just prior to cooking as they decompose very quickly and one dead one is a potential cause of food poisoning. If the mussels cannot be cooked on the day they are bought they should be kept in fresh cold water.

The mussels must be thoroughly cleaned before being cooked. First discard any which are open or cracked as these are probably dead. (Any that close on being tapped with the back of a knife are all right.) Scrub the remainder well. Cut off the beard and scrape off any loose barnacles. This should be done under running water. Rinse again in cold water until all the grit is removed.

Put the wine, water, bouquet garni and finely chopped shallot into a large pot. Cover and bring to the boil. Simmer for a minute or two until all the mussels have opened. Remove the mussels and take off the top shell. The sauce may at this stage be thickened with a little kneaded butter. Add chopped parsley to the sauce and pour over the mussels. Serve as quickly as possible.

Serving suggestion: Plenty of brown bread for mopping up!

Squid

Squid, known as *calmars* in French and *calamares* in Spanish, is a common Mediterranean fish. In Spain it is particularly popular and there are many different types. It can be very good if the squid are small and tender. The larger the squid generally the tougher and more chewy it is. Another advantage of buying the smaller squid is that they are also much easier to clean; so on all counts it is worth paying that little extra.

To clean squid, first pull the head part gently away from the body, which should remove a large part of the intestine. The tentacles, which are edible, should then be cut off just behind the eyes. This should, if done properly, leave the tentacles as a group. If the beak is still in the centre this must be thrown away with the remainder of the head and intestines. The body should then be turned inside-out and the inside thoroughly cleaned under running water. When this part of the operation is complete, turn the squid back the right way and peel off the skin on the outside. The ease with which this comes off depends on the type of squid. If the tentacles are large they, too, should have the outside skin taken off.

Calamares à la riojana

Cooking time 1¼-1¾ hours Working time 45-50 minutes

4 small squid
2 medium onions
1-2 cloves garlic
2 tablespoons olive oil

1 glass red, white or rosé wine
salt and pepper
bouquet garni
5-6 tomatoes

Clean the squid as described on page 96. Slice the onions and chop the garlic. Heat the oil in a saucepan and soften the onions and garlic. Cut the squid into rounds about ½ cm (¼ in) thick and throw in with the onions. Allow to fry for a minute or two, then turn up the heat and pour in the wine. Allow it to bubble for a minute, then lower the heat. Season with salt and pepper and add the bouquet garni. Cover the pan and cook very slowly for 1-1½ hours.

Skin and chop the tomatoes and cook in a little olive oil until they form a purée. Season well and add them to the squid mixture just before serving.

Serving suggestion: Serve with plain boiled rice.

Calamares mimosa

Cooking time 15-20 minutes Working time 40-45 minutes

2 tablespoons olive oil
3-4 cloves garlic, finely chopped

1 tablespoon finely chopped
  parsley
4 small squid
oil

Mix together the olive oil, finely chopped garlic and parsley and set aside to give the ingredients time to blend. Clean the squid and leave whole. In a frying pan heat a little cooking oil and add the squid. Fry for 10-15 minutes, turning the squid over from time to time. When all the oil has been used up and all the moisture has evaporated from the squid, pour the olive oil mixture over the fish. Fry the squid for a further few minutes in this mixture, then serve.

Calamares à la Romana

Cooking time 15 minutes Working time 30-40 minutes

4 small squid
flour

cooking oil for deep-frying
slices of lemon

Clean the squid as directed on page 96. Drain them well and cut into rounds about $\frac{1}{2}$ cm ($\frac{1}{4}$ in) thick. Leave again to drain. Flour them well and fry in very hot deep oil. Make sure the oil is hot by testing it with one piece of squid first. It should immediately froth up. Fried in this way the squid should turn out with a golden coating. Serve with slices of lemon.

7 Beans and pulses

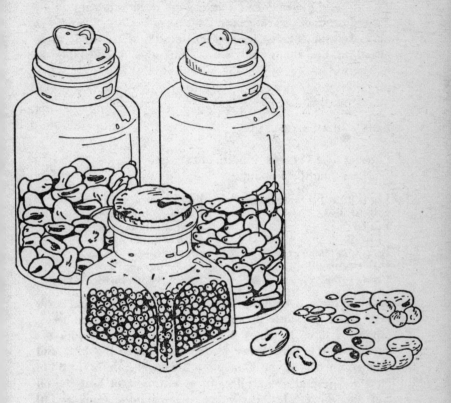

All these dried vegetables are ideal for cooking on top of the cooker. Until recent years, they have generally not been much used in English cookery but with the increased interest in vegetarian and foreign cookery there are now whole books devoted to cooking different types of beans. Unfortunately, within the confines of this book, I have not the room to give you more than a few recipes, some of which, like Chilli con

Carne are well known in various guises and others, like the Lentils with Chorizo, are less likely to have come your way, but all of which will I hope either introduce you to the possibilities of dried vegetables, or perhaps give you a few more ideas on how to cook them. All dried vegetables do, of course, need soaking and this is best done overnight or by leaving them all day, except in the case of lentils which need to be soaked for only an hour or so. If extra water needs to be added in the course of cooking, this should preferably be boiling water.

Spicy bean casserole

Cooking time 1½ hours + overnight soaking
Working time 10-15 minutes

¼ kg (½ lb) red *or* pinto beans
water *or* stock
1 onion
1 bayleaf
1 small tin tomatoes
1 tablespoon oil
1 clove garlic, crushed

1 dessertspoon tomato purée
1 chilli pepper, crushed
pinch of caraway seeds
pinch of cumin seeds
salt and pepper
paprika (optional)
½ green pepper, sliced

Soak the beans overnight. Rinse well. Put into a pan and cover with water or stock to about 1 cm (½ in) above the beans (approx ¾ litre, 1½ pints). Slice the onion and add with the bayleaf to the pan. Bring to the boil, lower the heat and simmer, uncovered, for 30 minutes. Meanwhile, drain the tin of tomatoes, reserving the juice. In a separate pan heat the oil and add the crushed garlic and the tomatoes. Cook for 10 minutes, then add to the beans with the tomato purée, the crushed chilli and the caraway and cumin seeds. Season with salt and pepper and a little paprika if desired. Continue cooking for another hour, then add the sliced green pepper for the last 15 minutes of cooking time.

Serving suggestion: Serve with a large bowl of dressed salad or perhaps with grilled gammon, bacon or sausages.

Chilli con carne

This dish is an old favourite and one for which most people have their own variations. Below I give one way of cooking this well-known Mexican dish. Personally, I always use pieces of braising steak rather than minced meat, although I know a lot of people use the latter. I do feel the chunks of meat are probably more authentic but it comes down in the end to a matter of personal preference.

Cooking time 2 hours + overnight soaking
Working time 20 minutes

150 g (6 oz) red *or* pinto beans
½ litre (scant pint) water *or* stock
1 tablespoon pork dripping *or* olive oil
¼ kg (½ lb) braising steak
caraway and cumin seeds (optional)
1 onion
1 clove garlic

1 teaspoon salt
1 teaspoon powdered chilli *or* 1-2 crushed chillis
1 dessertspoon sweet paprika
¼ kg (½ lb) tomatoes
chopped parsley

Soak the beans overnight. Rinse well and put in a pan with the water or stock and simmer, uncovered, for 45 minutes. Meanwhile, cut the meat into chunks. Heat the fat or oil in a frying pan and fry the meat until it is browned on all sides. If using caraway and cumin seeds add these at the same time as the meat. Slice the onion and chop the garlic. Add to the frying pan and fry until soft but not browned. Put the meat and onions into the pan with the beans and season with the chilli, paprika and salt. Simmer gently for another 45 minutes. Peel and chop the tomatoes, add to the stew and cook for a further 30 minutes. Serve with a liberal sprinkling of chopped parsley.

Casserole of beans and sausages

Cooking time 1¾ hours + overnight soaking
Working time 15 minutes

100-150 g (4-6 oz) red kidney *or*
 haricot beans *or* a mixture
1 onion, sliced
lard
¼ kg (½ lb) sausages
1 small tin tomatoes

125 ml (¼ pint) dry cider
125 ml (¼ pint) stock
1 teaspoon chilli powder
1 dessertspoon tomato purée
1 bayleaf
salt and pepper

Soak the beans in cold water overnight. Drain. Fry the sliced onions and sausages together in a little lard. When the onion is softened and the sausages lightly done, cut the sausages into halves or thirds and add all the remaining ingredients, including the soaked beans. Bring the mixture to the boil, lower the heat and cook, uncovered, for 1½ hours.

Serving suggestion: Serve with a green salad and fresh bread.

Haricot beans

Cooking time 1 hour + overnight soaking
Working time 5 minutes

200-250 g (8-10 oz) haricot beans
1 onion, sliced
1 carrot, sliced

1 bayleaf
salt and pepper
water

Soak the beans overnight. Drain and put in a saucepan with the sliced onion and carrot and the bayleaf. Season with salt and pepper. Cover with fresh water and cook, for 1 hour uncovered or until the beans are tender. Remove the onion, carrot and bayleaf, drain and serve.

Serving suggestion: These beans make a good accompaniment to sausage of any kind. A tomato sauce (see page 139) can be mixed in at the end.

Haricot beans with sweetcorn and bacon or frankfurters

Cooking time 1 hour 10 minutes + overnight soaking
Working time 10 minutes

200-250 g (8-10 oz) haricot beans
4-6 frankfurters *or* rashers of
  bacon

3-4 tablespoons cream
1 small tin sweetcorn
a few cumin seeds

Prepare the beans as in the previous recipe. If using bacon, fry this separately and then add this with the remaining ingredients to the drained beans. Heat through for about 5 minutes. If using the frankfurters, simply add these to the beans in the last 10 minutes of cooking before they are drained. Proceed as above.

Spinach potaje

Cooking time 1-2 hours + overnight soaking
Working time 20 minutes

100 g (4 oz) chick peas
1 litre (2 pints) water
½ kg (1 lb) spinach
25 g (1 oz) butter

1 tablespoon flour
1 egg yolk
salt and pepper

Soak the chick peas overnight, rinse and cook, uncovered, until tender in salted water for 1-2 hours. Clean the spinach and cook it for 7-8 minutes in the water in which the chick peas were cooked. Drain the spinach when it is ready, but reserve the water. Chop the spinach and pass through a vegetable mill. Melt the butter in a saucepan and stir in the flour off the heat. Return to the heat and cook over a low heat for a couple of minutes, then slowly add enough of the liquid reserved from the chick peas and the spinach to make a reasonably thick sauce. To this sauce add the pre-cooked chick peas and the prepared spinach. Beat the egg yolk with a tablespoon or so of water from the spinach. Add this to the pan, mix well and add more of the reserved liquid if the *potaje* is too dry. Adjust the seasoning.
Serving suggestion: Serve with pork, ham or sausages.

Lentils with bacon and parsley butter

Cooking time 1½ hours + 1 hour soaking
Working time 15 minutes

¼ kg (½ lb) brown or green lentils
1 onion, chopped
1 litre (2 pints) water
1 bayleaf
salt

¼ litre (½ pint) chicken or beef
  stock
4 rashers streaky bacon
large knob of butter
1 tablespoon chopped parsley
juice of 1 small lemon

Remove any pieces of grit from the lentils and soak in cold water for 1 hour. Drain and put into a pan with the chopped onion, a good litre (2 pints) of fresh cold water, the bayleaf and salt. Cook, uncovered, for 1¼ hours, by which time the water should have been absorbed or evaporated and the lentils tender. If this is not the case and extra water is needed it should be boiling. Any excess water remaining when the lentils are tender should be drained off. Add the chicken or beef stock and simmer until absorbed. Meanwhile, chop the bacon into small pieces and fry. Remove the lentils from the heat and add the butter, chopped parsley, lemon juice and bacon. Serve.

Lentils with chorizo

Cooking time 1½ hours + 1 hour soaking
Working time 10 minutes

¼ kg (½ lb) brown or green lentils
1 onion, chopped
1 litre (2 pints) water
1 bayleaf
salt

2 small serrano chorizos or
  2-3 cooked sausages
lard or oil
olive oil
vinegar

To prepare and cook the lentils proceed as in the previous recipe. Just before they are ready, cut up and fry the chorizo gently. Drain off any excess fat or oil remaining after frying as this has a very overpowering flavour and will spoil the flavour of the lentils. Serve the lentils with the chorizo sprinkled on top. On the table have oil and vinegar which each person can add according to taste. If this is not very convenient it can be added in the pan before serving. A dessertspoon of oil is about right for most tastes with a little more than half that amount of vinegar.

Cocido

This recipe is a simplified version of the Spanish *cocido* in which traditionally the dish provides 3 courses: a soup, a meat dish and the chick peas' served separately. However, certainly in bars it is rarely, if ever, served like that and this version is authentic if not traditional. It is a meal in itself and needs nothing to accompany it – except perhaps large quantities of red wine! I have given quantities for six people as it is the sort of dish that lends itself to large gatherings. It does keep perfectly well in the fridge for several days and is easily reheated.

Serves 6   Cooking time 3 hours + overnight soaking
Working time 20 minutes

½ kg (1 lb) chick peas	2 small serrano chorizos, sliced
1 bayleaf	3 morcillas *or* black pudding,
1 pig's trotter *or* ham bone	sliced
1 large onion, sliced	1 large potato, chopped
2 cloves garlic, chopped	2 large tomatoes, peeled and
1 tablespoon olive oil	chopped
1 teaspoon sweet red pepper	1 green pepper, sliced (optional)
(paprika)	

Soak the chick peas overnight. Drain, put into a large saucepan and cover with fresh water to about 1 cm (2 in) above the peas. Add the bayleaf, pig's trotter, sliced onion, chopped garlic, oil and red pepper. Cook, uncovered, for 1½-2 hours, then add the remaining ingredients and cook for another 45 minutes-1 hour. I find the addition of some sliced green pepper in the last 15 minutes adds a freshness and touch of colour to the dish.

8 Rice dishes

Rice is a very useful ingredient and is one of my 'basics' in the food cupboard. It is a lot more versatile than many people imagine, and can be used with other simple and easily available ingredients to form delicious hot supper dishes or made into interesting salads which need only be accompanied by a green salad to provide a summer lunch dish.

I refer in the recipe for Paella to a 'paella'. This is the pan in which the dish is made and is strictly a wide shallow metal pan with handles on either side. If you buy one of these in Spain you are quite likely to find it rusts easily, so it does need to be well dried and preferably kept oiled.

The other type of dish in which the rice dishes on the following pages can be cooked, and which I personally prefer, are the clay dishes which are used in Spain. These are glazed only on the inside, the outside being left unglazed. You can now find these in several stores in this country. They can go on direct heat but *must* be well soaked before using for the first time, otherwise they are liable to crack. They should also never be heated too rapidly, but as long as they are treated correctly they last for years. The advantage of these dishes is that, like the 'paella', they can be put straight on to the table.

If you are unable to obtain either of the utensils described above, then all the risotto-style dishes can be cooked in any frying pan.

To get rid of the excess starch in rice which is being used for a paella, the method favoured by most people of rinsing with boiling water is obviously useless. The way to deal with the problem when cooking these dishes is to rinse the rice several times in cold water before cooking.

You will notice in the following recipes that I have left the quantity of rice as a fairly vague measure. The reason for this is that in my experience the average 50 g (2 oz) per person is often insufficient if the people you are feeding are hungry! I always prefer to have more rather than less and any leftovers can be added to a stock (a stock cube will do) and made into a soup or puréed for the same purpose.

The quantity of water or stock is similarly vague, but for the additional reason that this is likely to depend on the quality of the rice and the presence of any other 'wet' ingredients, e.g. tomatoes. The golden rule here is to use less and add more if necessary, rather than having too much which makes the dish wet and mushy. Any water which is added should be boiling, otherwise if it is cold it tends to cause the grains to cook unevenly and give unsatisfactory results.

To make saffron rice, which I refer to as an accompaniment for several dishes, crush a pinch of saffron in a mortar and add a little boiling water. The solution, which will be a clear bright orange, should be added at an early stage to the boiling rice.

Paella

Paella is a very personal dish and it seems that each person has their own particular way of making it, which as far as they are concerned is the only way! Foreigners are certainly not expected to know how to make a *real* paella.

There are in fact two kinds of paella – one from Valencia and one from Alicante. The former is the one which most people associate with the name paella and contains shellfish as well as meat. The Alicante version does not contain any shellfish, only white meat such as chicken, pork and rabbit plus the traditional vegetables.

We found that in many cases the Spaniards don't always use proper saffron in paella, especially in the lower-class bars and restaurants, but merely something called *condimento amarillo,* which just means 'yellow condiment'. This accounts for the bright yellow colour often associated with paella. If saffron alone is used it gives a very delicate colour and flavour. For a little extra colour, a pinch of turmeric can be added.

Serves 4-6 Cooking time 1 hour Working time 1 hour

olive oil
2 chicken legs
water
salt and pepper
150 g (6 oz) frozen mussels
 or ½ kg (1 lb) fresh mussels
2 small artichokes (optional)
1 medium onion, chopped
2 cloves garlic, chopped
1 green pepper, chopped
350 g (12 oz) long-grain rice
good pinch of saffron
1 bayleaf
1 level teaspoon red pepper
¼ kg (½ lb) fresh *or* frozen prawns
100 g (4 oz) peas *or* Spanish beans
1 small tin red pimiento, sliced
wedges of lemon

In a pan heat enough olive oil to brown the chicken pieces. When they are browned on all sides drain off any excess oil and add water to almost cover the pieces. Season with salt and pepper, cover and cook for 25-30 minutes or until the meat comes easily off the bone. Reserve the stock for the paella.

If using fresh mussels, clean (see page 95) and then bring to the boil until they open. Take most of them out of the shells, reserving some for decoration in half-shells.

If using artichokes, cut off the stems and the tops, quarter and cook for 15 minutes in boiling salted water with a squeeze of lemon. This can be done in advance.

In a paella, heat any excess oil from the chicken and a good 3 tablespoons of olive oil. Fry the chopped onion, garlic and green pepper until soft. Add the rice and fry for a further 2-3 minutes before adding the stock, of which there should be twice as much as the quantity of rice. Grind the saffron in a mortar and add a little boiling water. The solution should be a clear bright orange. Add this to the paella with the bayleaf, salt and pepper and the red pepper.

If the prawns being used are fresh these should also be added at this stage. If they are frozen they should be added after 10 minutes, together with the mussels, chicken, peas or beans and artichoke quarters. The dish will be ready about 15 minutes after the stock has come back to the boil. 5 minutes before the end, arrange on top the sliced pimiento and the mussels in half-shells. Serve with wedges of lemon to squeeze over.

Serving suggestion: The Spaniards do not normally eat anything with paella except bread. If this seems like rather a lot of starch, try a green salad dressed with lemon juice and black pepper.

Note: The rice in paella should not be wet and the dish should be fast boiling all the time.

Mushroom and bacon risotto

Cooking time 25 minutes Working time 15-20 minutes

1 medium onion	$\frac{1}{4}$ litre ($\frac{1}{2}$ pint) stock
$\frac{1}{2}$ large green pepper	pinch of thyme
3-4 rashers bacon	1 bayleaf
1-2 tablespoons olive oil *or*	salt and pepper
sunflower oil	1 small tin sweetcorn, drained
100 g (4 oz) mushrooms	
100-150 g (4-6 oz) long-grain rice	

Slice the onion and green pepper finely. Remove the rind from the bacon and cut into pieces. Heat the oil in a paella or ordinary frying pan and in it soften the prepared ingredients. Meanwhile, slice the mushrooms. When the bacon is no longer transparent and the onion and green pepper softened, add the rice and fry gently for 2-3 minutes. Add the stock, mushrooms, thyme and bayleaf. Season with salt and pepper and cook, uncovered, until the rice is tender, about 15 minutes. The drained sweetcorn should be added in the last 5 minutes of cooking time.

Serving suggestion: Serve with a tomato salad (see page 153).

Milanese rice

Cooking time 25 minutes Working time 20 minutes

½ onion
3 *or* 4 tomatoes
50 g (2 oz) ham, bacon *or* chicken
olive oil *or* lard
100 g (4 oz) peas
1 bayleaf
½ teaspoon sweet red pepper
100-150 g (4-6 oz) long-grain rice

¼ litre (½ pint) boiling water
chopped parsley
40 g (1½ oz) grated cheese
knob of butter
½ teaspoon salt
1 tinned red pepper, sliced

Slice the onion and peel and chop the tomatoes. Dice the ham or bacon. Heat the oil or lard in a frying pan or preferably a paella dish, and soften the onion and bacon. If ham or cooked chicken are being used these can be added later. Once the onions are beginning to go golden, add the tomatoes, the peas (if they are fresh), bayleaf and the red pepper. After a couple of minutes add the rice and fry for a few minutes. Put in the water, a little chopped parsley, the cheese, the butter and the salt. Cook, uncovered, until the rice is tender, about 10-15 minutes. 5 minutes before the end of the cooking time, add the peas if they are frozen and arrange the sliced red pepper on the top.

Chorizo and rice

Cooking time 25 minutes Working time 20 minutes

100-150 g (4-6 oz) long-grain rice
1 onion
1 green pepper
1 tablespoon olive oil
2 small serrano chorizos
 or 2-3 cooked sausages
handful of French beans

3 tablespoons tomato purée
 (1-2 if it is the concentrated
 type)
1-2 cloves garlic, crushed
¼ litre (½ pint) boiling water
1 level teaspoon sweet red pepper
pinch of hot red pepper

Rinse the rice in several changes of water. Chop the onion and pepper (but not too finely), and fry until soft in the oil. Put in the rice and sliced chorizo and fry for about 2-3 minutes, then add the remaining ingredients. The beans should be cut up and preferably blanched before being added, otherwise they will not be quite cooked when the dish is ready. Cook, uncovered, for 15 minutes or until the rice is tender.

Chicken and rice

Cooking time 45 minutes Working time 15-20 minutes

1 piece of chicken (or leftovers)
olive oil or sunflower oil
¼ litre (½ pint) water
salt
1 bayleaf
½ onion
1 green pepper
1 red pepper (optional)
1 clove garlic

handful of raisins
1 large tomato
100-150 g (4-6 oz) long-grain rice
100 g (4 oz) peas
juice of ½ lemon
1 tinned red pepper, sliced for
 garnish

Fry the chicken in very little oil (preferably with the neck and feet also to make a good stock) until browned. Cover with the water, add a little salt and the bayleaf and cook fairly fast for 15-20 minutes. Meanwhile, chop the onion, green and red peppers and garlic and de-stone the raisins if necessary. Peel and chop the tomato. When the chicken is tender, remove from the bone and keep the stock. Fry the onion and peppers in about 1 tablespoon of oil until soft. Add the tomatoes, fry a further few minutes and then put in the rice. Stir for 1-2 minutes, then pour in the hot stock and add the remaining ingredients except the sliced, tinned red pepper. The peas should be added at this stage if fresh, if not they should be mixed in after about 10 minutes. Cook for a further 5 minutes. Garnish the dish with the sliced red pepper.

Tuna with rice

Cooking time 25 minutes Working time 15 minutes

1 onion	¼ litre (½ pint) stock *or* boiling
1 green pepper	water
1-2 tablespoons olive oil	1 bayleaf
freshly crushed black peppercorns	salt
3-4 tomatoes	1 small tin sweetcorn, drained
1 tin tuna fish, drained	(optional)
100-150 g (4-6 oz) long-grain rice	100 g (4 oz) peas
1 clove garlic, crushed	chopped parsley

Slice the onion and green pepper. Heat the oil in a paella or frying pan and sauté the onion and green pepper with a few crushed peppercorns. Meanwhile, skin and chop the tomatoes. Add these to the pan with the drained tuna, cook for a few minutes, then add the rice and the crushed garlic. Fry for 2-3 minutes, stirring occasionally, then add the stock, the peas if they are fresh, bayleaf and salt. Cook for 10 minutes, then add the drained sweetcorn and peas, if they are frozen. Cook for a further 5 minutes until the rice is tender and has absorbed all the water. Sprinkle with freshly chopped parsley.

Serving suggestion: Serve this with a bean shoots and orange salad (see page 153) which makes an unusual and interesting combination of flavours.

Rice with vegetables

This dish is really another variation on the same theme as the preceding recipes. Any vegetables can be used and the dish is therefore what you make it. Carrots, if used, should be sliced thinly and pre-cooked in the same water as the other vegetables.

Cooking time 30 minutes Working time 20 minutes

2 artichokes	25 g (1 oz) butter
lemon juice	100-150 g (4-6 oz) long-grain rice
½ small cauliflower	1 bayleaf
50 g (2 oz) French beans	pinch of turmeric
3-4 tomatoes	salt and pepper
1 small onion	50 g (2 oz) peas

Quarter the artichokes and cook them in boiling water with a little lemon juice. Remove any tough outer leaves. Break the cauliflower into small florets, slice the beans and cook these two vegetables together in salted water. When they are tender (you might find you have to remove the cauliflower first), drain, but reserve the water. Put aside these cooked vegetables. Skin the tomatoes and cut into slices. Chop the onion finely and sauté in the butter until softened. Add the tomatoes, cook for a few minutes, then put in the rice. Cook for 2 or 3 minutes, then add about 250 ml (½ pint) of the water in which the vegetables were cooked, the bayleaf and the turmeric. Season with salt and pepper. If using fresh peas, add these also at this stage. After about 10 minutes add the pre-cooked vegetables and, if using them, the frozen peas. Cook for a further 5 minutes.

Rice with sherry

Does the cupboard look rather bare? As long as the drinks cupboard contains something (even the remains of a bottle of wine) and you still have those perennial standbys, eggs and rice, try this dish.

Cooking time 25 minutes Working time 10 minutes

1 small onion	$\frac{1}{4}$ litre ($\frac{1}{2}$ pint) hot stock
1 dessertspoon oil	salt and pepper
100-150 g (4-6 oz) long-grain rice	1 dessertspoon butter
1 glass sweet *or* amontillado	
sherry *or* 1 glass white wine	2-4 eggs, hardboiled or fried

Slice the onion and sauté in the oil until softened. Add the rice and fry for 2-3 minutes, stirring occasionally. Pour in the sherry, then the stock. Cook for 15-20 minutes until the rice is tender. Season with salt and pepper and stir in the butter.

Serving suggestion: Serve with hard boiled or fried eggs and a green salad.

Pork and apricot rice

Cooking time 1 hour 10 minutes + overnight soaking
Working time 20 minutes

100 g (4 oz) dried apricots	150-200 g (6-8 oz) pre-cooked
1-2 tablespoons sugar	lamb or pork
25 g (1 oz) butter	2 rings pineapple
$\frac{1}{2}$ onion, chopped	salt and pepper
100-150 g (4-6 oz) long-grain rice	1 clove (optional)
$\frac{1}{4}$ litre ($\frac{1}{2}$ pint) stock	a little coriander

Soak the apricots overnight. Drain, cover with fresh water and add the sugar. Bring to the boil, lower the heat and stew gently until they are tender, about 45 minutes. Reserve the syrup. Cut the cooked apricots into small pieces.

Melt the butter in a paella or frying pan and soften the chopped onion for 5 minutes. Add the rice and fry for 2-3 minutes, stirring occasionally. Add the remaining ingredients, including several tablespoons of the syrup in which the apricots were cooked. Cook for 15-20 minutes.

Serving suggestion: Serve with celery, walnut and orange salad (see page 158).

Rice salad (1)

Cooking time 15 minutes Working time 15 minutes

100-150 g (4-6 oz) long-grain rice	2-3 tomatoes
olive oil	100 g (4 oz) peas
wine vinegar	1 green pepper
salt	½ onion
freshly milled pepper	½ tin tuna fish *or* any leftovers of chicken *or* ham

Cook the rice in plenty of boiling salted water. It is usually cooked about 10-15 minutes after the water has come back to the boil, although this depends on such factors as the quality of the rice, the amount of water etc. When cooked, the rice should be well drained and rinsed with boiling water to remove some of the starch and keep it light and fluffy. It is better, if anything, a little underdone for this recipe.

Season the rice while still hot with about 1 tablespoon of olive oil and 1 tablespoon of wine vinegar, extra salt if needed and some freshly milled pepper. While the rice is cooling, cut up the tomatoes into small dice and leave on a plate sprinkled with salt and pepper. Cook the peas. Finely chop the green pepper and onion. Mix all these ingredients with the rice and add the fish or meat.

Serving suggestion: Serve with a dressed green salad.

Rice salad (2)

Cooking time 15 minutes Working time 15 minutes

100-150 g (4-6 oz) long-grain rice	1 tinned red pepper, drained
olive oil	100 g (4 oz) mushrooms
wine vinegar	1 small tin sweetcorn, drained
salt and pepper	juice of ½ lemon
2 tomatoes	1 level dessertspoon chopped parsley

Cook the rice as in the previous recipe. Season the rice while still hot with about 1 tablespoon of olive oil and 1 tablespoon of wine vinegar, extra salt if needed and freshly milled pepper. While the rice is cooling, cut up the tomatoes into small dice, and finely chop the red pepper and the mushrooms.

Mix these ingredients with the sweetcorn, add the lemon juice, and add to the cooled rice. Sprinkle with chopped parsley.

Serving suggestion: Serve with cold meat or hardboiled eggs.

9 Pasta

Although I have given quantities and also cooking times for the pasta in the recipes below, for different reasons these are both variables: the former because it depends on the appetites of those who are going to be eating, and whether it is the main meal of the day or a starter, as well as the richness of the accompanying sauce; the latter because it depends on the quality and type of the pasta. However, by way of guidelines, about 200-250 g (8-10 oz) of pasta is right for two people as a main course, and as far as the timing is concerned, anything between 8-12 minutes, depending on the type of pasta being cooked, is about right. The only really reliable way of finding out whether pasta is cooked is by tasting it. It should be cooked enough to have lost its floury taste, but not so much that it is soggy and has lost its chewy quality. The Italian phrase is *al dente*. Pasta should always be immersed in large quantities of boiling water – about 2 litres (4 pints) is right for 200-250 g (8-10 oz) with just over ½ teaspoon of salt, and then simmered for the appropriate time. When it is cooked it should be rinsed in boiling water to get rid of excess starch, drained well and finished according to the recipe.

Spaghetti bolognese

Cooking time 40 minutes Working time 15-20 minutes

150 g (6 oz) purée of fried
   tomatoes
¼ kg (½ lb) minced beef
olive oil
1 large onion
1 large green pepper
2 cloves of garlic

spices: black peppercorns, sweet
   red pepper, nutmeg, cinnamon,
   oregano, thyme, ground clove
   and cayenne
2 glasses red wine
salt
1 bayleaf
200 g (8 oz) spaghetti
freshly milled pepper
knob of butter

First, make the purée of tomatoes. Peel and chop 6-7 tomatoes and fry gently in olive oil.

In a frying pan, brown the meat in a little olive oil. Chop the onion, green pepper and garlic and add to the meat. The spices should be prepared as follows: using approximately 6 black peppercorns, $\frac{1}{2}$ level teaspoon of sweet red pepper, large pinches of nutmeg and cinnamon, oregano and thyme and small pinches of clove and cayenne, grind these in a mortar to produce a fine powder. Sprinkle this mixture over the meat. When the onions and peppers are soft, add the purée of tomatoes, the wine, salt and bayleaf. If necessary, add a little water. Cook the sauce for 20-25 minutes.

Since the quality and type of spaghetti varies from brand to brand it is best to follow the instructions printed on the packet. However, the normal cooking method is: place the spaghetti in a large amount of boiling salted water and boil rapidly until soft, about 10-15 minutes. When the spaghetti is cooked, drain it thoroughly, season with freshly milled pepper and a knob of butter. Serve it on to the plates and cover with the sauce.

Note: Concentrated tomato purée or $\frac{1}{2}$ packet of powdered tomato soup may be used in place of the purée of tomatoes.

Carmela's macaroni

This is another recipe that was given to me by a Spanish woman. She was a cleaner at the place where I worked and is unable to read or write. However, I will testify to her ability to cook! The recipe as it was passed on to me made no mention of quantities, so those below are mine.

Cooking time 25 minutes Working time 15 minutes

1 onion	1 bayleaf
1 green pepper	salt and pepper
2 tablespoons olive oil	200-250 g (8-10 oz) macaroni
5-6 tomatoes	grated cheese

Cut the onion and pepper into small pieces and fry until soft in the olive oil. Skin and chop the tomatoes and add these with the bayleaf, salt and pepper. Cook well over a low heat. Cook the macaroni in plenty of boiling salted water for about 10 minutes. When it is ready, add to the prepared sauce with some grated cheese. Heat, stirring continually, until the cheese has melted.

Note: The fresh tomatoes can be replaced by tinned tomatoes or tomato purée.

Spaghetti carbonara

Cooking time 20-25 minutes Working time 20-25 minutes

200-250 g (8-10 oz) spaghetti	2 eggs
150 g (6 oz) streaky bacon	salt
50 g (2 oz) butter	freshly milled pepper
150 g (6 oz) mushrooms	2 tomatoes, sliced
½ small onion	chopped parsley

Cook the spaghetti in boiling salted water for 10 minutes. If using only one ring, drain and put aside. If using two rings prepare the remaining ingredients while the spaghetti is cooking. Remove the rind from the bacon and chop. Fry gently for a few minutes in half the butter in a saucepan or large frying pan. Slice the mushrooms and chop the onion very finely. Add the remaining butter to the pan with the mushrooms and onions. Cook for 5 minutes.

Beat the eggs in a bowl. Put the drained pasta into the pan with the onion, bacon and mushrooms. Season with salt and pepper. Add the egg and cook over a low heat, stirring constantly, until the egg is lightly set. Serve immediately, garnished with the sliced tomatoes and chopped parsley.

Spaghetti napolitano

Cooking time 30 minutes Working time 15 minutes

For the sauce:
½ kg (1 lb) tomatoes
½ onion
1-2 cloves garlic
1-2 tablespoons olive *or* sunflower
  oil

salt and pepper
oregano, basil

200-250 g (8-10 oz) spaghetti
knob of butter
grated Parmesan cheese

First, make the sauce. Skin and chop the tomatoes. Finely chop the onion and garlic. In a pan heat the oil and gently fry the onion until soft. Add the tomatoes and the garlic, and season with salt, pepper and a little oregano and basil. Cover and cook over a low heat until the tomatoes have reduced to a purée. Pass this purée through a vegetable mill, or *passe-puree*, and put aside.

Cook the spaghetti in boiling salted water for 10 minutes. Drain and toss in a little butter. Reheat the sauce, adjust the seasoning and serve over the spaghetti. Serve grated Parmesan cheese separately.

Spaghetti with sweet 'n' sour meatballs

Cooking time 45 minutes Working time 35 minutes

For the meat balls:
¼ kg (½ lb) minced beef
1 tablespoon cooked rice
½ onion, grated
½ clove garlic, crushed
1 egg, beaten
1 dessertspoon finely chopped
  parsley
salt and pepper

1 tablespoon oil *or* lard

For the sauce:
1-2 sticks celery, finely chopped
½ green pepper, chopped
5-6 fresh tomatoes, peeled and
  chopped
  or 1 small tin tomatoes
1 tablespoon cider, cider vinegar
  or wine
1 tablespoon brown sugar
salt and pepper

150 g (6 oz) spaghetti

To make the meatballs, combine all the ingredients and form into small balls about the size of walnuts. Sauté in the oil or lard until browned, remove and put aside.

To make the sauce, sauté the chopped celery and green pepper until tender. Add the remaining sauce ingredients and cook for 5 minutes, then return the meatballs to the pan. Cook for twenty minutes.

Meanwhile, in a large saucepan bring some salted water to the boil and cook the spaghetti for 10-15 minutes. Drain, add a knob of butter and some freshly milled pepper and serve with the meatballs and sauce on top.

Tagliatelle with prawns in sherry cheese sauce

An unusual, tasty and different way of serving both tagliatelle and prawns.

Cooking time 30 minutes Working time 15 minutes

1 clove garlic
20 g (¾ oz) butter
20 g (¾ oz) flour
1 glass amontillado sherry
¼ litre (scant ½ pint) milk, heated
salt and pepper
1 dessertspoon grated Parmesan cheese

25 g (1 oz) Cheddar cheese, grated
150 g (6 oz) shelled cooked prawns
4-6 nests tagliatelle verde
lemon wedges

Crush the garlic and fry gently in the melted butter. Add the flour, mix well and cook for 1 minute. Remove from the heat and pour in the sherry and then add the milk very gradually, stirring continuously with a wooden spoon. Season with salt and pepper. Return to the heat and cook gently for a few minutes, then add the cheeses and the prawns. The sauce, like any with the roux base, requires a certain amount of patience if it is not going to go lumpy.

Cook the tagliatelle in plenty of boiling salted water and serve with the prawn sauce. Garnish with lemon wedges.

Serving suggestion: A side salad of dressed lettuce makes a good accompaniment.

Tagliatelle with mushroom sauce

Cooking time 20-30 minutes Working time 20 minutes

½ small onion	1 tablespoon Marsala
100 g (4 oz) mushrooms	2-3 tablespoons chicken stock
2 rashers bacon	salt
25 g (1 oz) butter	freshly milled pepper
1 dessertspoon olive oil	4-6 nests tagliatelle
1 tablespoon flour	1 dessertspoon chopped parsley
oregano	

Chop the onion and slice the mushrooms. Remove the rind from the bacon and chop. Put the butter and oil in a pan and gently fry the onion and bacon for a few minutes. Add the mushrooms, cover and continue to fry gently for 5-10 minutes, then sprinkle over the flour and some oregano to taste. If, like me, you happen to be addicted to garlic, a little crushed garlic may also be added at this stage. Mix well and stir in the Marsala and the stock. Season with salt and freshly milled pepper. Cook for a further few minutes so that the flour taste disappears.

Cook the tagliatelle in plenty of boiling salted water, then serve the sauce over the pasta. Sprinkle with the chopped parsley.

Tagliatelle with tuna in cheesy corn sauce

Tinned food can be very useful to keep in the cupboard for the occasions when you need to 'rustle up' something out of nothing. This dish, although no doubt somebody somewhere has thought of it before, was the result of such an occasion.

Cooking time 15 minutes Working time 15 minutes

20 g (¾ oz) butter
20 g (¾ oz) flour
¼ litre (½ pint) milk, heated
25 g (1 oz) Cheddar cheese, grated
1 small tin sweetcorn, drained

1 tin tuna fish, drained
pinch of cayenne
freshly milled pepper
salt
4-6 nests of tagliatelle

Make a roux. Melt the butter gently, then stir in the flour off the heat. This should be done with a wooden spoon. Add the warmed milk by degrees over a low heat and continue stirring until bubbling. Add the grated cheese and cook for a further few minutes before adding the drained sweetcorn and drained tuna. Season with a little cayenne, freshly milled pepper and salt.

The sauce may now be removed from the ring whilst the tagliatelle is cooked in plenty of boiling salted water for 10-12 minutes, or it may be kept warm by the *bain-marie* method, i.e. standing in a pan of hot water.

Serve the sauce over the tagliatelle.

Pasta creole style

Cooking time 40 minutes Working time 20 minutes

200 g (8 oz) pasta shells *or* flat noodles
½ onion
25 g (1 oz) butter
4-5 good-sized tomatoes

½ green pepper
2 okra pods
100 g (4 oz) green beans, cooked
salt and pepper

Peel and chop the tomatoes. Chop the green pepper. Chop the onion and fry gently in the butter until softened, wash the okra, remove both ends, and slice. Parboil the noodles for 5-7 minutes in plenty of boiling salted water. Remove from the water, then blanch the okra by putting the slices into a sieve and dipping this for one minute into the water in which the noodles have been boiled. Add the tomatoes, green pepper, blanched okra and cooked beans to the onions in the pan. Season with salt and pepper and cook for 15-20 minutes, then add the parboiled noodles and cook until these are tender.

Pasta shells with cheese and mushrooms

Cooking time 15 minutes Working time 15 minutes

200 g (8 oz) pasta shells *or*
  macaroni
100 g (4 oz) mushrooms
50 g (2 oz) butter

75-100 g (3-4 oz) Cheddar
  cheese, grated
freshly milled pepper
salt

Cook the macaroni or pasta shells in plenty of boiling salted water for 10-15 minutes. While this is cooking, slice the mushrooms and sauté gently in the butter, covering them with a lid to retain the moisture. When the macaroni is ready, drain and rinse with boiling water. Add the grated cheese, freshly milled pepper, salt and prepared mushrooms.

Note: A little cream may be added to this dish just before serving, or for those garlic fanatics like myself, a chopped clove of garlic may be added to the mushrooms whilst they are cooking.

Cream pasta dish

Cooking time 25 minutes Working time 15 minutes

4 rashers bacon	1 small tin tomatoes
1 onion	1 tablespoon tomato purée
1 green pepper	salt and pepper
1-2 courgettes	2 tablespoons sweetcorn
100 g (4 oz) mushrooms	(optional)
knob of butter	200-250 g (8-10 oz) pasta shells
1 clove garlic, crushed	several tablespoons single cream

Remove the rinds from the bacon and dice. Chop the onion and green pepper. Slice the courgettes and mushrooms. Heat the butter and gently sauté the bacon, onion, green pepper and crushed garlic for 5 minutes. Add the courgettes and mushrooms and cook for a further 5 minutes. Put in the tinned tomatoes, the tomato purée and season with salt and pepper. Cook until the vegetables are tender, about 10-15 minutes, adding the sweetcorn in the last 5 minutes. Meanwhile, cook the pasta in plenty of boiling salted water. Remove the vegetable mixture from the heat and stir in the cream. Drain the pasta and mix this with the vegetable sauce. Serve.

10 Vegetables

The term covers a multitude of very different ingredients, from the common, often underrated and versatile potato, to such things as okra and chicory which many people are still unsure how to deal with. English cookery has, on the whole, tended to neglect vegetables and seen them only as an accompaniment to the meat dish. This is not the case in many other countries where vegetables are seen in their own right and cooked with imagination and care. Several of the dishes on the next few pages, such as Ratatouille, will probably be familiar to many of you, several of the others will not, but they are given as ideas and variations on the often boring theme of boiled vegetables and will, I hope, give inspiration for some possibilities of your own. Since we do not, as the French do, eat our various dishes separately, but put them all on one plate, I would suggest that if you are going to do a more unusual or exotic vegetable dish it is teamed with a plain meat dish.

Pommes frites

Pommes frites or chips to give them their more common name, are a very useful thing to do on a limited number of rings, as they can be cooked, put aside and then plunged back into the hot fat at the last minute. This was a trick learned from the owner/chef of a little restaurant where I worked for a few weeks one summer vacation.

2-3 large potatoes   salt (sea salt is good)
oil for deep-frying

Heat the oil (I nearly always use sunflower oil as it does not have the strong flavour of, say, corn oil) in a deep pan until it is very hot, but not smoking. Test it by dropping one of the chips in – if it bubbles and skids round on the top then the oil is ready. If it sinks to the bottom the oil needs to be hotter. Cook the chips until they are a very pale golden colour, then quickly remove with a draining spoon, put on to some kitchen paper and sprinkle with salt. They can then be left until you are ready to give them their final plunge into the hot fat. Follow the same procedure as before for testing the temperature of the fat, drop in the chips and within less than a minute they will be crisp and golden. Drain and serve.

Sauté potatoes

Cooking time 30 minutes Working time 10 minutes

¼ kg (½ lb) potatoes   salt and pepper
1 tablespoon oil   chopped parsley
25 g (1 oz) butter

Scrub the potatoes and boil in their skins. When they are tender, drain off the water, remove the skins from the potatoes (this is easier to do when they are hot, even if it does mean burnt fingers, rather than allowing them to get cold first) and slice. In a frying pan, heat together the oil and butter, add the potatoes and season with salt and pepper. Turn the potatoes occasionally until golden brown and crisp. Add a little extra butter if necessary. Sprinkle with chopped parsley just before serving.

Mousseline, puréed or creamed potatoes

These are all various names for what are basically plain mashed potatoes. The consistency of this dish is really a matter of personal choice although it would depend to some extent on the dryness of the dish it is to accompany. Accordingly, the quantity of milk is left vague. Creamed potatoes are best reheated in a *bain-marie*.

Cooking time 25-40 minutes (depending on size of potatoes)
Working time 10-15 minutes

¼ kg (½ lb) potatoes	salt and pepper
milk	knob of butter

Clean the potatoes. They may then be either boiled in their skins and the skins removed once the potatoes are cooked, or peeled first. Although most people do the latter and it is slightly easier than the former, if the skins are kept on the potatoes have a better flavour. Bring the potatoes to the boil in plenty of salted water. Boil until very tender. Drain and mash well with a fork. Heat the milk without boiling and add this to the potatoes until the desired consistency is reached. Season with salt and pepper to taste and add a knob of butter. Serve.

Patatas riojana

This dish is one I use for guests who take 'pot luck'. It comes from Northern Spain and was presumably originally made with wine from Rioja. It is cheap, tasty and simple and served with a green salad makes a very acceptable supper dish. It comes into the category of what I term rather loosely 'peasant dishes', and although it comes from a country where wine is cheaper than milk, there is no reason why, if you follow my recommendation of keeping remainders, or else a bottle of wine especially for cooking, you should not be able to rustle up this 'gourmet peasant dish' when the mood takes you. I have used a tin of tomatoes as it is an ingredient more likely to be easily available all the year round. It may of course be replaced by fresh tomatoes – I would suggest about ½ kg (1 lb) – which should be skinned and chopped.

Cooking time 40 minutes   Working time 15-20 minutes

1 large onion	¼ litre (scant ½ pint) stock
1 red or green pepper	2 glasses red wine
1 carrot (optional)	salt and pepper
4 good-sized potatoes	1 teaspoon Spanish paprika
1½ tablespoons oil	basil
1 large tin tomatoes	

Slice the onion, pepper and carrot. Peel the potatoes, wash and cut into thick slices. Heat the oil in a saucepan and gently soften the onion, potatoes, pepper and carrot for 10 minutes. Add the tinned tomatoes, the stock and the wine. Season with salt and pepper and paprika. A pinch or two of basil should be sufficient. Bring to the boil, lower the heat, cover and simmer gently for 30 minutes or until the potatoes are soft.

Spiced potatoes

This is another dish I discovered in Spain, which certainly transforms the old potato into something quite exotic.

Cooking time 30-40 minutes   Working time 10 minutes

¼ kg (½ lb) potatoes	1 dessertspoon sweet paprika
1-2 tablespoons olive oil	1 clove garlic
½ chilli pepper	1 teaspoon flour

Peel and slice the potatoes. Heat the oil in a pan and fry the chilli for 5 minutes, then remove it and put aside. In the same oil, fry the potatoes with the paprika sprinkled over. Cover the potatoes with water, add salt and cook, covered, for 20 minutes. While they are cooking, grind the garlic in a mortar with the fried chilli and the flour. Add a little cold water to make a paste, then a little stock from the pan. Pour this mixture into the pan, stir well and continue cooking until the potatoes are tender.

Serving suggestion: Serve these potatoes with a plain fried pork or lamb chop, with sausages or fried eggs.

Savoyarde potatoes

This dish is usually cooked in the oven, but as it is one of my favourite ways of cooking potatoes, I had to work out a way of doing it on top!

Cooking time 1 hour Working time 5 minutes

2 large potatoes
very small knob butter
40-50 g (1½-2 oz) Gruyère cheese,
  grated
1 clove garlic, crushed

150 ml (good ¼ pint) stock
  (½ stock cube + water)
salt
freshly milled pepper

Slice the potatoes, put the knob of butter in the bottom of a small saucepan and layer the potatoes with the cheese and crushed garlic. Pour the stock over and season with salt and freshly milled pepper, then use the *bain-marie* method to cook the potatoes with an all-round heat. Any wide open vessel half filled with water will serve the purpose. The potatoes will take about 1 hour or more to cook.

Serving suggestion: This dish is delicious with sausage of any kind, particularly the frankfurter type.

Carrots

Many English people cook carrots in lots of boiling salted water. The method I give below produces, I find, a much more tasty vegetable.

Cooking time 20 minutes   Working time 3-4 minutes

3-4 carrots, depending on size
knob of butter
salt

freshly milled pepper
chopped parsley

Slice the carrots and put into a pan with a little water (to cover the bottom) and the butter. Season with salt and freshly milled pepper. Cover with a lid and cook until the carrots are tender, being very careful they don't stick to the bottom of the saucepan. Mix in a little chopped parsley and serve.

Spinach

Cooking time 7-10 minutes Working time 5-10 minutes

Obtainable most of the year, spinach is easy to prepare and is a good accompaniment to either fish or meat dishes. It should be thoroughly washed and may then be cooked in one of two ways. It may either be put into a large pan of boiling salted water and boiled for 7-8 minutes, or put into a covered pan and cooked gently using only the moisture from the spinach itself and what is left on the leaves from washing it. As it cooks down very much you will need between ½ kg and ¾ kg (1-1½ lb) for two people. Drain well and when you are ready to use it, add a knob of butter, salt and pepper and return to the pan and reheat.

Seville spinach

Cooking time 15 minutes Working time 15 minutes

½ kg (1 lb) spinach	1 dessertspoon vinegar
½ small onion	2 slices white bread
¼ clove garlic	lard
butter *or* oil	cinnamon
½ teaspoon paprika	salt

Prepare the spinach according to the instructions given above. Drain and chop. Mince the onion and garlic together and sauté in a little butter or oil. Stir in the paprika and vinegar. Mix in the spinach, then cover and cook gently for 5 minutes. Meanwhile, fry the slices of bread in lard. When the spinach is ready, season with cinnamon and salt and serve with the fried bread.

Serving suggestion: Very good with poached egg.

Broad beans with ham, carrot and potatoes

Cooking time 50 minutes-1 hour Working time 10-15 minutes

1 tablespoon olive oil
100 g (4 oz) chopped ham *or*
  bacon
½ clove garlic, chopped
½ teaspoon sweet paprika
2 small new potatoes

2 carrots
½ kg (1 lb) shelled broad beans
¼ litre (½ pint) stock
½ glass white wine (optional)
salt and pepper

Heat the oil in a pan and fry the ham or bacon with the chopped garlic and the paprika for a minute or two. Slice the potatoes and carrots and add with the remaining ingredients to the pan. Bring to the boil, lower the heat, cover and simmer gently for 45 minutes-1 hour.

Serving suggestion: Serve with gammon or chicken.

Habichuelas trianeras
Green peas triana style

Cooking time 30 minutes Working time 20 minutes

½ kg (1 lb) small French beans
½ onion
¼ kg (½ lb) tomatoes
olive oil *or* pork dripping

4-6 tablespoons chopped bacon
½ clove garlic, crushed
1 bayleaf
salt and pepper

Top and tail the beans but leave them whole. Cook for 15 minutes, or until tender but still slightly crisp, in plenty of boiling salted water. Drain well. Slice the onion, peel and chop the tomatoes. Put about a dessertspoon of the oil or fat into the pan and fry the bacon pieces (for this kind of dish it is a very good idea to buy the offcuts which many butchers sell off cheaply). When the fat has turned colourless and the bacon pieces are rendering fat of their own add the onion and fry for 5 minutes until softened. Add the tomatoes, crushed garlic and bayleaf. Season with salt and pepper. Cover and cook for 10 minutes approx. As soon as the tomato/bacon mixture is well cooked toss in the beans, heating through if necessary. Serve.

Note: The amount here makes a pleasant light supper or lunch dish followed perhaps by some cheese. If, however, it is to be used as an accompaniment to a meat dish (it goes very well with either pork or chicken) this amount will do for four people.

Peas à la Espanola

This is in fact very similar to Petits Pois à la Francais, the idea in both being to use the moisture from the lettuce in which to cook the peas and add extra flavour. Fresh or frozen peas can be used for this dish.

Cooking time 10-15 minutes frozen peas, 20-25 minutes fresh peas
Working time 5 minutes

½ onion	¼ lettuce
1-2 rashers bacon	350 g (12 oz) peas
25 g (1 oz) butter	salt and pepper

Chop the onion and bacon finely and sauté in the butter. Cut the lettuce into strips and add with the peas to the pan. Season with salt and pepper. Cover tightly and cook until the peas are tender.

Artichokes

Cooking time 25 minutes Working time 5-10 minutes

This recipe was given to me by a Spanish woman and resembles all Spanish recipes I have ever received in that no quantities are mentioned. As in this case I don't see that it matters too much, I give it here in (almost) its original form.

Put some oil in a saucepan. When it is hot, add onions cut into pieces and fry until they are golden. Then throw in some breadcrumbs and the juice of a lemon, then the artichokes cut into pieces, salt and a little water and cook covered for 20 minutes.

Artichokes can be served either cold with a vinaigrette sauce or hot with a sauce boat of melted butter or melted garlic butter, if they have been simply cooked in boiling water for about 40 minutes.

Note: If you haven't had much to do with artichokes I should explain that there are two kinds, globe or leaf artichokes and Jerusalem artichokes. The kind mostly seen in Spain are the leaf artichokes, which is what the recipe is for. Even if they are small it is best to remove the outside leaves and cut off the top. The stalk should also be cut off to level the base. As the base of the leaf and the heart are the edible parts of the vegetable a plate should be provided for the remainder of the leaves, although if the artichokes are young many Spaniards eat the whole of the leaf as in the recipe above.

Fried peppers

Cooking time 20 minutes Working time 10-12 minutes

Choose smallish green or red peppers. Wash and dry them well and cut in half if necessary. In a frying pan heat 2 tablespoons of olive oil. Put in the peppers and cook, slowly turning over at intervals to make sure they are softening. After 10 minutes cover with a lid and cook for a further 10 minutes or until they are well browned, wrinkled and soft. Sprinkle with coarse salt and serve.

Serving suggestion: These peppers make an excellent accompaniment to any plain fried meat.

Ratatouille

One of the French women I worked for was an absolute perfectionist, and insisted that to cook ratatouille all the ingredients should be cooked separately first and only combined later. This may well be the case, but is not really a very practical proposition for most of us unless making large quantities! However, ratatouille is a dish that keeps very well and is in fact often tastier the day after it is made than on the same day. For this reason, and also because of the preparation involved I do think it is worth making more than the bare minimum. It is also vital that olive oil is used. Aubergines, in particular, absorb a lot of oil and using a different kind does not give the same flavour.

Serves 4 Cooking time 1 hour 20 minutes Working time 20 minutes

2 courgettes	3-4 tablespoons olive oil
2 aubergines	½ kg (1 lb) tomatoes
2 medium onions	salt and pepper
2 green *or* red peppers	chopped parsley
2 cloves garlic	

Wash and slice the courgettes and aubergines into pieces about 2 cm (1 in) long. Slice the onions and peppers and chop the garlic. Heat the oil in a pan large enough to contain all the ingredients and fry the onion and garlic for 5 minutes. Add the courgettes, aubergines and peppers. Fry for a further 5 minutes, adding extra oil if necessary. Cover and cook for 30 minutes. Meanwhile, peel and chop the tomatoes. After 30 minutes add these and season with salt and pepper. Cook for a further 40 minutes over a low heat. In the finished dish the various vegetables should all be distinguishable. Sprinkle with chopped parsley.

Serving suggestion: A very good dish to serve with pork or veal.

Stuffed peppers

Cooking time 45 minutes-1 hour   Working time 20-25 minutes

For the stuffing:
1 tablespoon fine breadcrumbs
1 clove garlic, crushed
½ small onion, minced
1 dessertspoon chopped parsley
a little grated nutmeg
1 egg
¼ kg (½ lb) minced beef *or* pork
salt and pepper

4-6 peppers depending on size
flour
oil

For the tomato sauce:
1 onion, chopped
6 medium tomatoes, peeled and
   chopped
cumin seeds
salt and pepper

To make the stuffing, mix together the breadcrumbs, garlic, onion, parsley, nutmeg. Beat the egg with a fork and blend well with the meat. Mix in the other ingredients and season with salt and pepper.

Once the stuffing is prepared, cut off the tops of the peppers and remove the seeds. Stuff them with the meat mixture. Dip the open ends in flour and fry the peppers in hot oil until the skin begins to wrinkle.

To make the tomato sauce, fry the chopped onion in oil until soft, add the peeled and chopped tomatoes and a few cumin seeds. Season with salt and pepper. Simmer for 15 minutes, then sieve. Pour this sauce over the peppers and cook, covered, for 30 minutes.

Note: This mixture can be used to stuff tomatoes, courgettes and aubergines as well as peppers.

Menestra

This is a very versatile vegetable dish which can be varied according to the vegetables in season. I give below one possible version and leave it to your imagination and preferences to invent the variations.

Cooking time 30-35 minutes Working time 10-15 minutes

½ onion	1 clove garlic, crushed
1 carrot	salt
1 tablespoon olive oil	knob of butter
2-3 tomatoes	50-100 g (2-4 oz) peas
100 g (4 oz) green beans	sprig of mint
1 courgette	

Slice the onion and carrot and fry gently in the olive oil. Chop the tomatoes. Top and tail the beans and cut in half. Cut the courgettes into quarters lengthwise and then into pieces about 2 cm (1 in) long. When the onion is beginning to soften, add the beans, tomatoes, courgettes, crushed garlic, salt and the butter. The peas should be added if they are fresh. If they are frozen they should be added after a further 15-20 minutes when the sprig of mint should be included for the last 5 minutes of cooking. The dish is ready after 20-25 minutes, depending on when the beans and carrots are tender.

Corn on the cob

Cooking time 10-15 minutes Working time 2 minutes

Sweetcorn is grown in this country and is also imported. It is in season from August to late September. When choosing sweetcorn to cook on the cob it should be remembered that when the grains are bright yellow and squashed together the corn is past its best and is likely to be tough and to have lost its delicate flavour. The grains should be a pale yellow colour.

To prepare the corn, cut off any bottom stalk and strip away the leaves. Cook in boiling salted water for 10-15 minutes, depending on how young and tender the corn is. Drain well and serve with salted butter.

Corn on the cob is usually eaten with the fingers, although small forks that can be stuck into either end are sometimes used. If using fingers, a finger bowl is not a bad idea!

Mexican style corn

Cooking time 10-15 minutes Working time 5-10 minutes

½ onion	knob of butter
1 clove garlic	1 tinned red pimiento, chopped
½ green pepper	1 small tin sweetcorn, drained
½ fresh green chilli	

Chop the onion, garlic, green pepper and chilli and fry gently in the butter until softened. Add the chopped pimiento and the drained sweetcorn and heat through for 5 minutes.

Serving suggestion: This is a very good vegetable dish to serve with plain fried meat or meat done *sofrito* style. It is also very good with omelettes.

Note: For those who like their food hot, the whole chilli may be added. It may also be omitted – but then the dish ceases to be Mexican.

Stuffed cabbage leaves (1)

This is a Hungarian version of a dish popular in most Middle Eastern countries.

Cooking time 1 hour 20 minutes Working time 20 minutes

For the stuffing
oil *or* lard
50 g (2 oz) long-grain rice
150 ml (6 fl oz) stock
½ small onion, chopped
1 teaspoon chopped parsley

½ egg, beaten
¼ kg (½ lb) minced pork

4-6 cabbage leaves
4-6 rashers streaky bacon
1 small onion, chopped
soured cream .

Melt a little oil or lard in a pan and fry the rice for a couple of minutes, then add a little stock. Boil until the rice is tender. Drain and reserve the stock. Whilst the rice is cooking, pour boiling salted water over the cabbage leaves and let them stand for 15 minutes.

Brown the chopped onion in a little oil or lard, adding the chopped parsley in the last few minutes. Remove from the heat. Blend with the beaten egg and add the minced pork and rice.

Drain the cabbage leaves and place in the middle of each a large spoonful of stuffing. Fold both ends inwards and roll the leaves round the stuffing. Around each roll wrap a rasher of streaky bacon and tie with cotton or use small skewers.

Melt a little oil or lard in a casserole, put in a layer of chopped onion, add the cabbage rolls and cover with the reserved stock. Cook for at least 1 hour and then thicken the gravy with a few spoonfuls of soured cream. Adjust the seasoning and serve.

Stuffed cabbage leaves (2)

This is a Greek version of the dish and was given to us by an American Greek who was living in Spain. The difficult part is the accompanying sauce which requires great care and patience.

Cooking time 1 hour Working time 20-25 minutes

For the stuffing:
50 g (2 oz) long-grain rice
¼ kg (½ lb) minced lamb
1 tablespoon chopped parsley
¼ teaspoon cinnamon
salt
freshly milled pepper

4-5 large cabbage leaves
water
juice of 1 lemon
salt
For the sauce
2-3 eggs
juice of 1-2 lemons

To prepare the stuffing, put all the ingredients into a bowl and knead well until thoroughly blended. Prepare the cabbage leaves as in the previous recipe and roll them round the stuffing. Line a saucepan with spare leaves to prevent the rolls from sticking and lay the stuffed leaves on top. Cover with water and add the lemon juice. Add a little salt to the water. Cover the pan with a tight-fitting lid and cook gently for 1 hour.

Just before the stuffed cabbage leaves are ready, prepare the sauce. This is quite a tricky operation although the ingredients are so simple. Whisk the eggs in a saucepan over an *extremely* gentle heat. This is the sort of occasion when a small piece of asbestos is very useful to spread the heat evenly. Continue whisking the eggs until they are stiff and frothy and then begin to add the lemon juice, little by little. The sauce must remain smooth and not be allowed to turn into a type of lemon scrambled egg! Continue whisking gently over the heat until the lemon has all been added and the sauce is smoothly cooked. Put the *dolmades* on to the plates and pour the sauce over immediately.

Provençal style mushrooms

I owe this recipe to one of my employers in France. It was almost invariably served with escalope of veal or fillet steak.

Cooking time 15-20 minutes Working time 15-20 minutes

2 shallots	2 tomatoes
1 clove garlic	salt and pepper
150 g (6 oz) mushrooms	small pinch of rosemary
1 tablespoon olive oil	a little lemon juice

Chop the shallots finely. Crush the garlic with a little salt. Clean the mushrooms either by rinsing briefly under running water, or rubbing gently in a damp cloth. Do not peel but slice finely. Fry the onion and garlic for 5 minutes in the oil, then add the mushrooms and fry for a further 5 minutes. Peel and chop the tomatoes, and add to the ingredients in the pan. Season with salt and pepper, add the rosemary and fry for a further 5 minutes. Squeeze over a little lemon juice before serving.

Note: This dish is easily reheated.

Fried lemon cauliflower

Until a few years ago, I had always assumed that the only way of cooking cauliflower was to boil it and was quite surprised when an American friend served it to me cooked in the following way.

Cooking time 25 minutes Working time 15 minutes

½ cauliflower *or* 1 small cauliflower	½ green pepper, sliced (optional)
olive oil	juice of ½ lemon
a good teaspoon paprika	a little water

Break the cauliflower into very small pieces. Heat a little oil in a small pan which has a lid and put in the pieces of cauliflower and the paprika. Fry over a gentle heat for 5 minutes. Add the sliced green pepper, if you are using this and fry for a further 5 minutes, then add the lemon juice and a little water. Cover the pan and cook over a gentle heat for 10-15 minutes or until the cauliflower is tender, being careful to ensure that there is always sufficient water in the pan to stop the cauliflower 'catching' on the bottom.

Braised celery

Cooking time 45 minutes-1 hour   Working time 20 minutes

1 heart celery	25 g (1 oz) butter
½ onion	100-150 ml (¼ pint) stock
1 carrot	bouquet garni
	salt and pepper

Wash and trim the celery, (reserving the leaves if wished as a flavouring for stock or soup). Cut the celery into pieces about 4-5 cms (2-3 in) long. Dice the onion and carrot finely. Blanch the celery for a few minutes in boiling salted water, then drain. Melt the butter in a pan and in it gently fry the onion and carrot for 2-3 minutes. Add the celery and pour in the stock and the bouquet garni. Season with salt and pepper. Cover and cook gently for 45 minutes-1 hour or until the celery is tender. The liquid will reduce during cooking but more may be added, if necessary.

Serving suggestion: This vegetable dish goes well with a plain meat dish or a dish with similar ingredients such as braised lamb.

Braised chicory

Chicory is one of those vegetables regarded by many English people with suspicion. Most people have heard it is bitter and are somewhat put off. It need not be, and cooked the following way makes a tasty and slightly unusual vegetable accompaniment to a meat dish.

Cooking time 30-45 minutes Working time 5 minutes

4 heads chicory
100-150 ml (¼ pint) chicken stock
12 capers

a little lemon juice
small knob of butter
salt and pepper

Trim the bottom of each head of chicory and take off any outside leaves that do not look fresh and crisp. Rinse the heads under cold water and wipe dry. Place the chicory heads in a shallow pan and pour over the stock. Sprinkle in the capers and a little lemon juice. Add the knob of butter and season with salt and pepper. Cover and cook slowly for 30-45 minutes until the chicory is tender. Serve with the juice from the pan spooned over.

Courgettes in cheese sauce

Cooking time 15 minutes (sauce) + 10 minutes Working time 20 minutes

¼ litre (½ pint) milk
20 g (¾ oz) butter
20 g (¾ oz) flour
grated cheese
salt

freshly milled pepper
lemon juice
6 small courgettes
chopped parsley

Make a bechamel sauce by first heating the milk in a small saucepan. Melt the butter in another thick-bottomed saucepan until it is foaming. Remove from the heat and add the flour, mixing well. Add a little of the warmed milk and stir until a thick paste is formed. Return to a very low heat and cook gently, gradually adding the rest of the milk, stirring carefully all the time so that no lumps are formed. Continue cooking until the sauce no longer tastes of flour. Add grated cheese to taste and season with salt and pepper. A squeeze of lemon juice at this stage gives an added interest to the sauce, which should be of a creamy consistency. If it is not, a little more milk may be added.

Now prepare the courgettes by washing them and then, depending on size, either quartering or halving lengthwise and cutting into pieces about 4 cm (1½ in) long. I find the pieces retain their firmness better this way than if cut into rounds. Cook with a little salt, a little water and a knob of butter in a covered saucepan. When tender, but not mushy, sprinkle with chopped parsley. Reheat the sauce by the *bain-marie* method, i.e. by placing the saucepan containing the sauce into a larger pan containing boiling water. Pour the sauce over the courgettes.

Vegetable fritters

Cooking time 10 minutes Working time 20 minutes

1 egg	oil *or* fat
50 g (2 oz) flour	1 small can sweetcorn, sliced
150 ml (¼ pint) milk	aubergine, green pepper, mixed
salt and pepper	cooked vegetables etc.

Beat together the egg, flour and milk to make a smooth batter. Season with salt and pepper. If possible leave to stand for 30 minutes. Then, if using sweetcorn or cooked diced vegetables, add these to the batter and drop by spoonfuls into the hot fat. (Test the fat by dropping in a test spoonful of the mixture. It should whizz round on the surface.) If coating something like slices of aubergine, mix these into the batter and drop each slice into the fat. Fry until nicely browned all over, then drain well on kitchen paper.

Serving suggestion: These fritters go well with fried chicken.

Okra with tomatoes

Okra is not a particularly common vegetable as far as English kitchens are concerned. It is of tropical Asian origin, but is common generally in the southern hemisphere and goes under a great many names. The other name by which it is most frequently known in English is ladyfingers. One of the most usual ways of cooking it is with tomatoes.

Cooking time 40 minutes Working time 40 minutes

1 small onion	100 g (4 oz) okra pods
½ clove garlic	1-2 tablespoons olive oil
½ green pepper	1 teaspoon brown sugar
½ fresh chilli pepper (optional)	squeeze of lemon juice
2-3 tomatoes	salt and pepper

Chop the onion, garlic, green pepper and chilli. Peel and chop the tomatoes. Wash the okra, and cut off the ends. Heat the oil in a frying pan and sauté the okra until browned, then remove from the pan. In the remaining oil, adding a little extra if necessary, sauté the onion, garlic, green pepper and chilli until the onion is lightly browned. Add the tomatoes, sugar and lemon juice. Season with salt and pepper and cook, covered, for 5-10 minutes until the tomato is well blended. Return the okra to the pan and cook for a further 5 minutes or until the okra is tender.

Serving suggestion: Serve with rice or haricot beans. Also very good as a vegetable with steak or pork chops.

Braised lettuce

Braised lettuce is used in France as a dish for slimmers. It does, however, also make a very good accompanying vegetable. The lettuces should be firm-headed and may be left whole with the outer leaves removed. Alternatively, it can simply be treated in the same way as spinach or cabbage and torn up.

Cooking time 20-25 minutes Working time 10 minutes

1-2 lettuces
25 g (1 oz) butter
1-2 tablespoons beef stock
   (optional)

salt and pepper
ginger (optional)

Wash the lettuces thoroughly. If leaving the heads whole, wash them by spreading the leaves as much as possible and plunging repeatedly head first into the water. Drain. Melt the butter in a pan, add the lettuce and the beef stock if using this. This is not strictly necessary as the lettuce will produce enough moisture of its own. Season with salt and pepper. Cover and cook over a low heat for 20-25 minutes if using the whole heads, or 10-12 minutes if the lettuce is in leaves. Remove the lid for the last few minutes to allow some of the moisture to evaporate. A Chinese friend of my sister's always sprinkles a little ginger over at this stage, which does add an interesting flavour.

11 Salads

With the growing number of health food and vegetarian restaurants around now, and the increasing interest in the preparation of food, the days of a salad being a piece of wilting lettuce, a quarter of a tomato and a few slices of cucumber thrown on to a plate are, thank goodness, becoming a thing of the past. The lettuce and tomato remain, of course, as indispensable basics, but to go with them are some suggestions to add a variety of colour, tastes and textures to your salad days.

Vinaigrette

If your salads are to be interesting it is vital that you should be able to make a good vinaigrette. Vinaigrette is one of those many things in cookery where each person seems to feel that his or her recipe is the only real way of doing things. If you have already found your favourite way of making this dressing, fine; for those who haven't may I suggest several things. Firstly, if you can always use olive oil and wine vinegar. The quantities of oil to vinegar tend to be a matter of personal preference, although I was told quite categorically by one French cook that they couldn't be anything other than 3:1, I find this fine for a lettuce dressing, but tend to reduce the ratio to 2:1 for a dressing for tomatoes and cucumber. The only other essentials for a vinaigrette are the salt and pepper. Things like dry mustard powder, garlic and sugar are all optional. The dressing can be made up in 'bulk' and kept in a jar or made each time you wish to use it. Either way, the oil and vinegar should be well mixed so that they form a creamy suspension.

Green salad

To the French, *une salade verte* is a salad of dressed lettuce only. This can be amplified by the addition of slices of green pepper and cucumber if desired. A little thinly sliced onion may also be added.

Wash and tear up the lettuce. (Using a knife bruises the lettuce.) Always make sure the lettuce is dry before using it in any salad. If you haven't got a proper drier, kitchen paper can be very useful. The dressing should be made at the bottom of the bowl, which may be rubbed with a clove of garlic if you do not wish to put any in the dressing itself. The salad should always be tossed at the last minute before serving.

Salade niçoise

Working time 15 minutes

radishes
1 lettuce
2-3 tomatoes
½ tin French beans
black olives
1 small tin anchovy fillets

a few capers
vinaigrette dressing (see page
    151)
1 small tin tuna
1 hard-boiled egg

If you want to make this dish look decorative, prepare the
radishes by cutting each radish into halves using a series of
diagonal cuts into the centre. You should have at the end a
circle of two-sided triangles which will give each half a jagged
edge when they are separated. Leave these in cold water until
the tips of these 'petals' bend outwards giving a flowerlike
impression. Meanwhile wash and tear up the lettuce and cut
up the tomatoes. Drain the beans, the anchovy fillets and the
tuna, reserving the oil from the tuna to add to the vinaigrette if
desired. Put the lettuce into a glass bowl, add the tuna and
some of the tomatoes and beans. On top arrange the anchovy
fillets, olives, radishes and grated hard-boiled egg with the
remainder of the tomatoes and beans. Sprinkle over a few
capers and pour over the vinaigrette.

Mixed salad

Simply add a few tomatoes, some green pepper, cucumber,
onion and perhaps some celery to the basic green salad.

Tomato salad

Slice several good firm salad tomatoes and half a smallish onion. Mix well with some vinaigrette. Unlike a green salad, a tomato salad improves with standing in the dressing for a while. If you have access to some basil add a little of this to the salad, if not, some chopped parsley is a good addition, or occasionally for a change a little chopped mint is refreshing.

Bean shoots and orange salad

1 orange
1 small punnet of bean shoots

a few peanuts (optional)
vinaigrette dressing (see page 151)

Peel and segment the orange. Cut the segments into halves or thirds and put into a bowl with the washed bean shoots. Add the peanuts and pour over the vinaigrette.

Tuna or chicken and pasta salad

Cooking time 10-15 minutes Working time 10 minutes

200 g (8 oz) pasta shells
1 dessertspoon olive oil
1 teaspoon vinegar
½ green pepper
2 tablespoons sweetcorn
1 small tin tuna fish
  or 2 tablespoons cooked chicken

2 tablespoons cooked peas
1 dessertspoon mayonnaise
salt
freshly milled pepper

Cook the pasta in plenty of boiling salted water (see page 120). Drain well, and while still hot mix in the oil and vinegar. Whilst it is cooling chop the green pepper. Add all the remaining ingredients to the pasta and season to taste with salt and freshly milled pepper.

Serving suggestion: Serve with a green salad.

Note: If using the tuna rather than the chicken for this dish, you may prefer to omit the extra oil and simply use the oil in the tin with the tuna. In this case mix the tuna and the oil in with the pasta whilst the pasta is still hot.

Celery and carrot salad

Working time 5 minutes

3-4 sticks celery	a little lemon juice
1-2 carrots	salt
1 dessertspoon mayonnaise	freshly milled pepper

Cut up the celery as small as possible and finely dice the carrots. Put into a small salad bowl and mix in the mayonnaise. Squeeze over lemon juice to taste. Season with salt and freshly milled pepper.

Serving suggestion: This simple little salad is very good with hardboiled eggs.

Gipsy salad

Working time 5 minutes

2 tinned red peppers	a few black peppercorns
2 green peppers	2 cayenne peppers
½ small onion	1 tablespoon olive oil
2 cloves garlic	1 tablespoon red wine vinegar
1 heaped tablespoon grated carrot	hot paprika
	salt

Finely chop the peppers, onion and garlic and put into a bowl with the grated carrot. Crush the peppercorns with one of the cayenne peppers in a pestle and mortar (the other one goes in whole). Mix with the oil, vinegar, paprika and salt. Pour this over the ingredients in the salad bowl. Allow to stand for 2-3 hours.

Note: This salad is very hot!

Tuna salad

Working time 5 minutes

1½ tablespoons olive oil
½ tablespoon lemon juice *or* wine vinegar
1 clove garlic, crushed or chopped (optional)
½ onion

1 green pepper
3-4 large tomatoes
1 tin tuna fish
salt
crushed peppercorns
chopped parsley

Pour the oil into a salad bowl, then add the lemon juice or vinegar and amalgamate well. If using garlic, add at this stage. Dice the onion finely and slice the green pepper into rings or strips, depending on its shape or size. Slice or chop the tomatoes. Put all these into the salad bowl with the tuna and any oil from the tin. Mix well, so that the tuna is not in large lumps. Season with salt and the crushed or very coarsely milled peppercorns. Sprinkle with chopped parsley.

Cucumber salad

Working time 5 minutes

1 tablespoon olive oil
½ tablespoon red wine vinegar
1 clove garlic
½ onion
1 green pepper

½ small cucumber
2 tomatoes
1 teaspoon sweet paprika
a little hot paprika *or* cayenne
salt

Mix the oil and vinegar together well in a salad bowl. Chop the garlic finely and put into the vinaigrette. Dice the onion and green pepper and slice the cucumber and tomatoes finely. Put these into the bowl and season with the peppers and salt. This salad has a much better flavour if left to stand for an hour or two before serving.

Coleslaw

Working time 5 minutes

½ apple
1 small onion
1 large carrot
½ small Dutch cabbage
a few raisins

juice of 1 small lemon
2 teaspoons good mayonnaise
salt and pepper
hot paprika (optional)

Chop the apple very finely. Dice the onion, also very finely, and grate the carrot. Cut up the cabbage into small strips. Put all these ingredients into a bowl with a few raisins. Pour the lemon juice over the contents of the bowl. Mix in the mayonnaise and season to taste with salt and pepper. I usually add a little hot paprika to give extra flavour.

Avocado winter salad

Working time 5-8 minutes

50 g (2 oz) white cabbage
2 sticks celery
2 carrots
15 g (½ oz) shelled walnuts
1 tablespoon grated onion

1 tablespoon wine vinegar
2 tablespoons olive oil
salt and pepper
dry mustard (optional)
1 ripe avocado

Cut up the cabbage finely and slice the celery. Wash the carrots and cut into thin sticks. Roughly chop the walnuts. Put all these ingredients into a bowl with the grated onion. Mix the vinegar with oil and season with salt and pepper. A little dry mustard may also be added if desired. Peel and dice the avocado and toss in the dressing, then add both to the salad.

Serving suggestion: Serve with hardboiled eggs, cheese or cold meat.

Greek salad

Working time 10 minutes

½ small lettuce	black olives
1 small onion	2 tablespoons olive oil
1 small green pepper	a little lemon juice *or* wine
2 large tomatoes	vinegar
2-3 tablespoons white cabbage	salt and pepper
a few slices of cucumber	50 g (2 oz) feta cheese

Wash and dry the lettuce and chop finely. Slice the onion and green pepper into rings. Slice the tomatoes and cut up the cabbage. Arrange these ingredients on two plates with the slices of cucumber and sprinkle with a few black olives. Pour over the oil and a little lemon juice, then season with salt and pepper and crumble the feta cheese over the top.

Cottage cheese special

This recipe makes a very good party dip or a tasty accompaniment to a salad.

Cooking time 10 minutes Working time 5 minutes

1 hardboiled egg	cayenne pepper
2 tomatoes	paprika pepper
1 large tub cottage cheese	salt
1 tablespoon mayonnaise	chopped chives *or* parsley
	(optional)

Chop the hardboiled egg and slice the tomatoes finely. Put the cottage cheese into a bowl and mix in the mayonnaise, hardboiled egg and tomato. Season to taste with cayenne, paprika and salt and add chopped chives or parsley if desired.

Celery, walnut and orange salad

Working time 5-10 minutes

4 sticks celery	1 tablespoon olive oil
½-1 orange, peeled	1 tablespoon white wine vinegar
1 tablespoon walnuts	or ½ tablespoon vinegar and ½
freshly milled pepper	tablespoon lemon juice
	salt or pepper

Cut the celery into pieces about 2 cm (1 in) long. Segment the orange and cut the segments into halves or thirds. Chop the walnuts roughly. Put these ingredients into a bowl and over them grind some black pepper. Do not waste any of the juice which may come from the oranges when cutting them up – pour it from your chopping board over the salad! In a small bowl or jug mix together the oil and vinegar and season with salt and pepper. Pour over the salad.

Note: If possible, this salad should be prepared a few hours before it is to be eaten – this gives the orange flavour time to permeate the salad.

12 Desserts

Although I think my first real interest in cookery arose through making cakes and desserts, nowadays I rarely make either. I used to take great delight in making gateaux or mousses for my mother's dinner parties and decorating them with great care (something she was more than delighted to let me do), but somehow now I prefer concocting a main course or even a starter. This may have something to do with the fact that when cooking for just one or two desserts do not seem to feature largely in the menu, or it perhaps has to do with the diet that

I, for one, am always about to start. Anyway, whatever the reason, the fact remains that desserts no longer feature prominently in my repertoire. Because of this and also the fact that many of the more elaborate desserts require an oven, all the desserts in this chapter are extremely simple, but are the kind that invariably go down well. Old favourites like chocolate mousse and fruit salad are always acceptable. In several cases I have given quantities for four on the basis that most of these are for dinner party type desserts and not the sort of thing you will want to turn out every day.

Caribbean bananas

Cooking time 10 minutes Working time 10 minutes

2 large *or* 4 small bananas	brown sugar
35 g (1½ oz) unsalted butter	1 tablespoon dark rum
a few raisins ·	

Cut the bananas in half lengthwise. Melt the butter in a small frying pan. Put in the bananas and the raisins and fry gently until the bananas have changed colour (they go a deeper yellow). Sprinkle over sugar to taste. Warm the rum in a soup ladle and light it before pouring carefully over the bananas. Shake the pan a little until the flames have died down.

Serving suggestion: Serve with cream or ice-cream.

Note: This dish can be served and flambéed at the table as long as the rum is hot before it is lit.

Chocolate mousse

Serves 4 Working time 10 minutes

4 eggs
4 oz melted bitter chocolate
  (112 g *or* approx 18 squares of
  a 150 g block)

Separate the egg yolks from the whites. Melt the chocolate in a dish or pan placed over hot water. Beat the yolks into the melted chocolate. While allowing this mixture to cool slightly, whisk up the egg whites until they are stiff enough to stand in peaks and then fold into the chocolate mixture. This dessert looks best served in individual dishes and should be chilled slightly before serving. Cream can be whipped or simply poured over, although the mousse is just as delicious without.

Fruit salads

Fresh fruit salad is one of the simplest, and to my mind, one of the pleasantest of desserts. It has almost infinite variations and most people have their preferences. It also depends, of course, a great deal on the season and the availability of the fruit. Here I give two possible combinations.

Winter fruit salad

Working time 5 minutes

1 orange	nutmeg
1 banana	ground clove
½ apple	½-1 level dessertspoon sugar
½ grapefruit	sweet sherry (optional)
cinnamon	

Peel and cut up the fruit and put it all together in a bowl; a glass bowl looks best. Sprinkle sparingly with the spices and add the sugar, and a little sweet sherry.

Summer fruit salad

Working time 5 minutes

1 orange	juice of 1-2 lemons
½ apple	sugar
1-2 peaches	1 tablespoon water
strawberries	

Cut up all the fruit and put it into a bowl. Pour the lemon juice over the fruit. Sprinkle with sugar according to taste and add the water. Chill before serving.

Spanish rice pudding

Serves 3-4 Cooking time 20 minutes Working time 20 minutes

1 litre (2 pints) water	peel of ½ orange
100 g (4 oz) round-grain rice	peel of ½ lemon
salt	cinnamon
½ litre (1 pint) milk	½ cinnamon stick
100 g (4 oz) sugar	

Bring the water to the boil and add the rice with a pinch of salt. Bring back to the boil and boil for 3 minutes. Drain and rinse the rice with cold water. In another pan bring the milk, sugar, orange and lemon peel to the boil. Add the rice, mix well and cook for 20 minutes, being careful not to overdo it. Put it into a glass bowl or individual dishes, sprinkle with a little cinnamon and decorate with pieces of cinnamon stick. Leave to cool before serving.

Crème caramel

This is basically a simple recipe, but it is not always easy to turn out successfully. Most people seem to have their own preferred method of making it, both as regards the caramel and the custard mixture. Below I give one possible method.

Serves 4-6 Cooking time 55 minutes Working time 20 minutes

150 ml ($\frac{1}{4}$ pint) water	$\frac{1}{2}$ litre (1 pint) milk
100 g (4 oz) sugar	25-45 g (1-1$\frac{1}{2}$ oz) sugar
3 eggs	1 vanilla pod *or* $\frac{1}{2}$ teaspoon
1 egg yolk	vanilla essence

Put the water and sugar in a thick-based pan. Over a low heat dissolve the sugar, stirring occasionally with a wooden spoon. When the sugar has dissolved, bring to the boil and boil without stirring until the sugar has turned a rich, golden brown. Have ready some lightly oiled dariole moulds or one large mould and coat these all round with the caramel. Leave until set. Beat the eggs and the egg yolk. Heat the milk with the sugar and pour it on to the beaten eggs. If using a vanilla pod, this should be put into the milk and left to infuse for about 10 minutes (it should then be removed, dried and stored for further use in a jar of castor sugar) before the milk is slowly poured on to the eggs. If essence is used this may be added at any stage. Pour the mixture into the moulds and cover with greased paper or kitchen foil. This prevents a skin forming on the surface of the custard. Cook by the *bain-marie* method, that is in a saucepan with water in it to come nearly to the top of the mould(s). The water should be hand-hot when poured in and should on no account be allowed to boil as this could cause the custard to curdle. The custard will take 45 minutes-1 hour to cook, depending on whether you are using a single or individual moulds. To test, insert a fine skewer; if it comes out clean the custard is ready. Leave to cool a little before turning out.

Oranges in caramel sauce

Cooking time 20 minutes Working time 20 minutes

4 good oranges	brandy *or* Grand Marnier
5 tablespoons water	(optional)
100 g (4 oz) loaf sugar	whipped cream
125 ml ($\frac{1}{4}$ pint) orange juice	

Remove the rind from one orange, cut into julienne strips and boil it for 5 minutes in the water. Leave to stand for a further 5 minutes, then remove the peel. In the water dissolve the sugar and add the orange juice. Boil the sugar, water and juice mixture until there is a thickish golden syrup. A tablespoon of brandy or Grand Marnier can be added to the syrup for extra flavour. Peel the oranges, removing all the pith, and arrange in segments in a glass bowl. Pour over the syrup and top with whipped cream. The thin julienne strips of peel that have been softened in the water can be used for decoration.

Syllabub

This is a very traditional old English dessert, which is extremely simple to make and ideal for dinner parties.

Working time 10 minutes + several hours marinading

thinly pared rind of 1 lemon	150-200 ml ($\frac{1}{4}$ pint) double cream
juice of 1 lemon	grated nutmeg *or* chopped nuts
3 tablespoons white wine	*or* grated lemon rind
1 tablespoon brandy	sponge fingers
30 g (1 oz) castor sugar	

Put the lemon rind into a bowl with the lemon juice, wine and brandy. Leave for several hours or overnight. Strain into a large bowl, add the sugar and stir until dissolved. Slowly add the cream, stirring all the time and then whisk until the mixture forms soft peaks. Spoon into sundae glasses and sprinkle with nutmeg or nuts or, if wished, finely grated lemon rind. Serve with sponge fingers.

Zabaglione

Zabaglione can be served either hot or iced, according to taste.

Cooking time 15 minutes Working time 15 minutes

2 egg yolks	$\frac{1}{2}$ glass Marsala *or* sweet sherry
50 g (2 oz) castor sugar	

Beat together the egg yolks and sugar in a pan over low heat until poached and frothy. Stir in the Marsala or sherry. Serve in glasses immediately if it is to be served hot. If it is to be iced, continue beating until it is cold and mix in 2-3 tablespoons whipped cream before chilling in the refrigerator.

Apple froth

Cooking time 10-15 minutes Working time 15 minutes

3-4 dessert apples *or* 2 cooking
  apples
1-2 dessertspoons brown sugar
1 small egg white
1 tablespoon whipped cream
  (optional)

1 tablespoon orange juice
1 dessertspoon lemon juice
1 tablespoon castor sugar
pinch of cinnamon

Peel, core and slice the apples. Put into a pan with a little water and cook until softened. Add brown sugar to taste. Whip the egg white until it just stands in peaks and fold into the purée. Add the whipped cream, the orange and lemon juice and the sugar. Season with a pinch of cinnamon to taste. Spoon the mixture into sundae glasses and decorate with extra whipped cream if desired.

Chestnut cream

Serves 6 Working time 10 minutes

½ litre (1 pint) cream (double or
  whipping)
450 g (14-16 oz) tin chestnut
  purée

2 tablespoons castor sugar
3 tablespoons brandy
75 g (3 oz) chocolate

Whip the cream until it is thick but not quite standing in peaks. Fold three-quarters of the cream into the chestnut purée and add the sugar and brandy. Mix well and spoon into sundae glasses. Top with the remainder of the whipped cream. Melt the chocolate and spoon over just before serving.

Note: This is a very rich dessert so it is not advisable to serve it after a heavy main course.

Lemon cheesecake

Despite its name, this delicious sweet contains no cheese at all, and is delightfully simple to make.

Serves 4 Working time 15 minutes Chilling time 1 hour

For the flan case:
digestive biscuits
unsalted butter

For the filling:
150 ml (¼ pint) fresh cream
1 small tin condensed milk
1-2 lemons

Crumble enough biscuits to line your flan case (normally about three-quarters of a small packet). This is best done on a flat surface with a rolling pin. Rub in enough butter, about 40-50 g (2 oz), to bind the crumbs and press this mixture into the flan case.

Whip the cream until stiff and fold in the condensed milk. Grate in the rind of the lemons, then squeeze them and pour in the juice. Spread this filling on to the base in the flan case and chill in the fridge for at least 1 hour before serving.

Strawberry or raspberry yoghurt sorbet

Serves 4 Working time 15 minutes Chilling time 2-3 hours

¼ kg (½ lb) raspberries *or*
  strawberries
75 g (3 oz) castor sugar
¼ litre (½ pint) natural yoghurt

juice of ½ lemon
4 tablespoons water
15 g (½ oz) powdered gelatine
2 egg whites

Rub the fruit through a sieve to make a thick purée. Add the castor sugar, then stir in the yoghurt and lemon juice. In a small cup or bowl put 4 tablespoons water and sprinkle over the gelatine. Allow it to stand for 5 minutes before putting the bowl over a pan of hot water and stirring until the gelatine has dissolved. Add the gelatine to the purée. In a separate bowl beat the egg whites until they stand in peaks and fold into the purée mixture. Spoon the mixture into a container, cover and put into the freezer. When it is about frozen, remove from the freezer, beat it up with a whisk, then return to the freezer to set firmly. Remove from the freezing compartment to the fridge about 2 hours before serving.

Blackcurrant ice-cream

Serves 2-3 Working time 20-25 minutes
Chilling time several hours

$\frac{1}{4}$ kg ($\frac{1}{2}$ lb) blackcurrants   100 g (4 oz) icing sugar
1 dessertspoon lemon juice   150 ml ($\frac{1}{4}$ pint) double cream

Rinse the fruit and, if necessary, strip from the stems. Press the fruit through a fine sieve, or put into a blender to make a purée. Stir in the lemon juice and sieve in the icing sugar. Beat up the cream until it stands in peaks, then fold into the puréed blackcurrant mixture. Pour into a container and place, uncovered, in the freezer. As it freezes, turn the sides into the centre occasionally and stir around. Then cover and freeze until firm for several hours. Transfer to the fridge to soften slightly about 30 minutes before serving.

Menu ideas

Prawn Cocktail
Steak in Cream Sauce
Fruit Salad

★★★

Potage Bonne Femme
Kidneys with Mushrooms,
Peppers and White Wine
Chocolate Mousse

★★★

Stuffed Eggs
Castilian Lamb
Apple Froth

★★★

Grapefruit
Spaghetti Bolognese
Crème Caramel

★★★

Melon
Veal in Orange
Spanish Rice Pudding

★★★

Consommé al Jerez
Beef or Chicken curry
Strawberry Yoghurt Sorbet

Chilled Cucumber Soup
Pork in Cider
Syllabub

★★★

Curried Eggs
Chicken Fricassee
Oranges in Caramel Sauce

★★★

Gazpacho
Paella
Iced Zabaglione

★★★

Tomato Soup
Goulash
Caribbean Bananas

★★★

Tuna Salad
Coq au Vin
Strawberries and Cream

★★★

Salade Niçoise
Catalan Fish
Lemon Cheesecake

Index

Book Tokens

Give them the pleasure of choosing

Book Tokens can be bought and exchanged at most bookshops in Great Britain and Ireland.